EVERYONE LEAVES BEHIND A NAME

TRUE STORIES

Everyone Leaves Behind a Name: True Stories.
By Michael Brick

Cover Design by: Stravinski Pierre and Siori Kitajima,
SF AppWorks LLC http://www.sfappworks.com
Formatting by Siori Kitajima and Ovidiu Vlad for SF AppWorks LLC
E-Book Formatted by Ovidiu Vlad

Cataloging-in-Publication data for this book
is available from the Library of Congress.

ISBN-13: 978-0-9964901-5-3
ISBN-10: 0-9964901-5-9

Published by The Sager Group LLC
info@TheSagerGroup.net
info@MikeSager.com

EVERYONE LEAVES BEHIND A NAME

TRUE STORIES

BY MICHAEL BRICK

THE SAGER GROUP

Artibus Te Adiuva

For Stacy, Sadie,
John-Henry,
and Celia

An absolutely necessary part of a writer's equipment, almost as necessary as talent, is the ability to stand up under punishment, both the punishment the world hands out and the punishment he inflicts upon himself.

—Irwin Shaw

TABLE OF CONTENTS

Foreword by Dan Barry /// ix

PART I. PEOPLE

3 /// A Hipster Quits Williamsburg, and Gets a Haircut

7 /// Tracing Steps of the Man Who Walked Away

13 /// Dusk of the Drummer

17 /// New Orleans Arena League Team Casting Quite a Spell

23 /// Jingo Unchained

35 /// Brisket Bandit Exposes Flaw: Justice System Struggles
to Stop Repeat Offenders

43 /// Art or Vandalism? An Austin Detective Follows the Trail
of a Graffiti Artist Known as "Kudos"

53 /// Ex-N.F.L. Star Dreams of Taking Sports to Space

59 /// Awaiting Millions, Brother Fights for Sister, Their Home

PART II. PLACES

67 /// Where Summer Glides Down Like a 9 A.M. Beer

73 /// Finding Shade in a Legend's Shadow

77 /// Last Call on the Boardwalk, Perhaps Forever

81 /// Where Doves, and the Threat of Danger, Fill the Air

87 /// In Busted Boomtowns, Ministers Seek Troubled Souls

95 /// Longhorn, Sooner Fans Experience Different Twist
to Weekend Revelry

99 /// Austin's Franklin Barbecue is All the Rage,
and Long Lines are a Daily Ritual

PART III. OCCURRENCES

107 /// Night That Girl, 7, Died Is Recounted In Family Court

111 /// Undercover Agent in Real Fur Snares a Fake Veterinarian

115 /// Sorority of the Swamp

123 /// The Big Race

153 /// Old New Yorkers, Newer Ones, and the Line Etched
       by Sept. 11

161 /// Life Without Parole for Killer of a Police Officer

165 /// Given Five Extra Years to Live, New Yorkers Look for a Catch

171 /// The Distributor

Acknowledgements /// 184

About the Author   /// 186

About the Publisher /// 187

FOREWORD

One of the side benefits of the writing career is how it keeps you in the conversation. Those writers known as journalists, though, tend not to dwell on this truth. They will talk about the honor of bearing witness, the thrill of holding the powerful accountable, the dopamine rush from stumbling upon a juxtaposition of words that creates sparks in the mind. In moments of acute self-regard (at, say, yet another writing conference's awkward cocktail gathering), they will declare that "It's all about the story"—the utterance of which should banish the speaker to actuarial work, so damnably precious is the sentence.

But writers know that the achievements of the actuary go unheralded, the heroics of the soldier lost in war's mist, the art of the hairdresser rinsed away by the first shower. The work of the gifted journalist, however, lives on, his words pressed into paper, her phrases aglow on a laptop screen. In some mysterious way, their every story says to the future: I am here beside you, and I have a tale to tell.

Mike Brick is one of those writers who never leaves your side, and what pleasurable company he provides. As you will discover from this collection of his newspaper and magazine journalism, his words create sparks that flash in the night sky of the mind like fireworks.

In reading these stories from Brooklyn, Houston, and beyond, picture the man. Tall and lanky and so proud to be Texan. Declaring his Lone Star-ness to all of Gotham during his tenure at *The New York Times*, wearing a brown vest and cowboy boots, and taping a Cormac McCarthy quotation to the wall above his desk. Using the telephone to beguile a subject one moment, and the next to express his dismay—his wounded-to-the-soul disbelief!—that some editor did not want to join him in telling a story differently, and why is this editor even in the business if not to tell the tale of the human condition afresh, goddam.

Then out the door to another story, the narrow reporter's notebook in his back pocket slapping at his flat ass, as if urging him onward because these blank pages needed filling. Brick fills them all right, his slanting, elongated scrawl capturing all that he sees and hears in courthouses and at precinct stations, in dark bars and at swanky parties, along sun-blinding beaches and from snow-blessed mountaintops.

The words of Brick breathe life into his subjects. Here is Willy, the world-weary lady bartender at a salt-air bar, and all you need to know is that "Her daddy was William, who wanted a son." Here is Minerva Ramirez, aging with Down syndrome, her hair tied in a floral bow, "pretty like Tinkerbell." And Danny Wimprine, a talented quarterback too small for the N.F.L., who throws women-swooning touchdowns for the New Orleans VooDoo arena football team. And Peter Carmine Gaetano Napolitano, the bartender at the Melody Lanes bowling alley in south Brooklyn, wearing suspenders and a red-trimmed cummerbund, "an insurance policy for pants."

Thanks to Brick, they too sit beside you. So make room for the Coney Island mermaids, wearing green-sequined bras and knocking back Buds. Another round, please.

Lingering as well are those Brickian phrases. A child murderer's gaze "like an empty lot." A bar being "a mystery no one wants to solve." A veteran bartender looking "made out of old tires and paste." Yes.

When accused of overwriting by those who could not write at all, he wrote—or overwrote—an impassioned defense of literary risk-taking:

"That word, though, if it is a word: Overwritten. In recent years it's become a sledgehammer in the hands of too many cowardly, unambitious, ladder-climbing, cow-in-a-swivel-chair editors. The good ones know how to tell you where to dial it back, and finding a good one is mission critical. I've been lucky in that regard. The bad ones are hanging a kneejerk, uninspired, boardroom groupthink scarlet O on stylish writing."

The occasional overreach, if it does occur, is a small tax to pay for the many payoffs—for being able to read, say, that a bouncer was "built like an upturned piano." Pitch-perfect phrases like this come from the synthesis of risk and rigor, a willingness to leap and then take a step back, and sometimes maybe only a half-step.

Imagine, then, Brick's internal dialogue as he pushes and checks, pushes and checks:

> This word is almost right, but not quite. This word is glorious, but it does not belong here. This phrase, oh my God, this one phrase is positively at one with the moment, but Gawker will say it's too much, Gawker will mock me to the delight of all the professional mockers on the sidelines of life. They will accuse me of overwriting and their mockery will live on in Internet infamy.
>
> Fuck Gawker.

Time and again in this collection and in his other work—including two non-fiction books—Mike Brick takes risks and delivers. He has, of course, the good writer's requisite ear for language, the facility for words. But he also possesses uncommon courage, coupled with uncommon wisdom.

"Fools believe in final sentences," he once wrote, and how beautiful is that. Make room beside you.

— Dan Barry

PART ONE: PEOPLE

A Hipster Quits Williamsburg, and Gets a Haircut

The story of Mr. Todd Fatjo's departure from his truly dope duplex loft is one of those rare pieces that manages to capture a subculture in a moment of transition, and were that all the story did, it would be a success. Most people wouldn't have seen a flier and understood that modern anthropology begins, and often ends, with noticing something hiding in plain sight. In this recognition, and the mental hop-scotch from there to the wide angle lens, Michael Brick shows his reporting virtuosity. But there's something else, a subversive undercurrent laced beneath the story, managing to both be a newspaper trend piece while also subtly poking fun at the entire conceit. The voice and language is confident, and reading it always makes me picture a young man, running flat out and roaring, in complete control. Even the use of The New York Times' honorific isn't perfunctory; he turns a stodgy rule of style into another weapon in his arsenal. There's a line by singer-songwriter Jason Isbell that comes to mind when I get to the last sentence about building the city on rock n roll: "A vandal's smile," Isbell sings, and that's what I imagine on Brick's face when he finished typing this dispatch. He'd completely captured a world, avoiding the tropes so common with similar trend stories, and while evoking hipster Brooklyn and Mr. Fatjo's transition from a DJ to "some guy with a job," he'd left behind a finger in the eye of those who'd sling cartoons and clichés. He wrote a flawless story, while managing to spray-paint his name on the worst impulses of journalists, doing both at the same time. It is nearly perfect.

—Wright Thompson

DATELINE: Brooklyn, New York

Todd Fatjo has moved out, and Williamsburg may never be the same.

New York neighborhoods do not announce their sea changes. There is no news release or banner draped across the street. Sometimes there is just a certain guy, and a thing that guy does, and before you know it the neighborhood has made one of those subtle shifts, the sort that keep New York City fascinating.

Remember when Bill Clinton opened an office in Harlem? Or when Miguel Algarin founded the Nuyorican Poets Cafe on the Lower East Side? Or when Harvey Lichtenstein started spreading the Brooklyn Academy of Music facilities around Fort Greene?

Todd Fatjo is no former president or renowned poet, but for Williamsburg he is a tiny bellwether. In this neighborhood, bohemianism begat or gave way to hipsterism in the blink of a decade, and Mr. Fatjo was right there.

One moment, there were industrial lofts illegally housing art students who spent days at the L Cafe. The next, there was not one but two cavernous Thai restaurants, and the neighborhood kept them both busy.

And there was Mr. Fatjo, in an expansive loft far from the main drag, Bedford Avenue, knee-deep in the hoopla. He had a job at a record store, gigs as a D.J., an untamed Afro and three roommates. They held five parties during their tenancy that Mr. Fatjo would later describe as major, defined as involving three separate sound systems blaring away in different parts of the apartment.

"It was just insane," Mr. Fatjo said.

The telltale sign that the party was ending came in the hipster equivalent of semaphore: a flier on a wall. Inside the shopping mall on Bedford Avenue, below the flier for the dance band seeking a musician, Mr. Fatjo posted notice earlier this summer that the partying-est loft in all of Williamsburg was on the market.

He wrote with a simple yet passionate eloquence, speaking directly to his peers in a parlance that showed him to be of the place and moment.

"If you've ever been to my duplex loft you know how truly dope it is," Mr. Fatjo began. He listed some conventional real estate amenities, such as wood floors, 14-foot ceilings and skylights for a monthly rent of $2,400, then moved on to recount others that only a steeped Williamsburg hipster could appreciate:

"Popeye's and Dunkin' Donuts on the corner, about four 24hr bodegas on the corner, 2 Chinese food places next to both entrances, and it's above and across from two $.99 stores," he wrote.

If you have to ask why proximity to multiple 99-cent stores might be an advantage, you will never know. Mr. Fatjo's truly dope duplex loft is not in the gentrified Williamsburg of investment bankers and corporate media types. Those 24-hour bodegas he mentioned have bulletproof glass, and one sells Marlboros with Virginia tax stickers. This is the Williamsburg where a spoonful of party helps the squalor go down.

There are other things you will never know if you did not live in Williamsburg through the heydays of bohemians and hipsters, and Mr. Fatjo invoked that secret knowledge in his flier.

"Every party we've had was one for the books," he wrote. "If you've been to one, you know, if not you missed out."

Again signaling his connection to the heart and soul of modern Williamsburg, Mr. Fatjo concluded his flier with a tone of solemn inconsequence, of utter detachment from the whole matter.

"So I guess if anyone is interested leave a message or call me," he wrote, adding his cellphone number and e-mail address.

Lest the neighborhood be left in confusion and suspense, Mr. Fatjo tacked on a postscript hinting at what the future might hold for the young and insufferably hip.

"BTW:" Mr. Fatjo wrote, abbreviating by the way, "The only reason I'm leaving is because my girlfriend and myself want to get a place to ourselves and this place is too big."

Love is a funny thing. It can spin a cynical hipster around like a record (baby, right round, round, round), and it has done a number on Mr. Fatjo, who is 28. He quit the music store this year and took a job showing apartments in Manhattan. He is working toward a broker's license, and this month he had the Afro shorn to a nice, respectable wave.

Mr. Fatjo and his girlfriend took up residence in the South Bronx, but despite all the changes in his own life, he was surprised to find that the party seems to be ending for his generation of Williamsburg hipsters. He had written the flier to help find a new tenant because he was fond of the landlord, but the hipsters he had expected never showed interest.

"I was trying to get some friends in here who were D.J.'s or artists, because you can do whatever," Mr. Fatjo said. "The demand for it wasn't what I thought it would be."

Last week, the landlord rented the loft to a tenant from another apartment in the same building, a man who had never joined the hipster parties.

"He's just some guy who has a job," Mr. Fatjo said.

The fate of the truly dope duplex loft may be a sign that the hipster scene is fading in Williamsburg, or who knows? Some new generation could reinvigorate the neighborhood with its own brand of cool. As for Mr. Fatjo, who is fast becoming just some guy who has a job, the end of the party is bittersweet.

"It really kills me to leave Brooklyn, especially this place," he said, dwelling on a last look around the empty loft. "But doing something with my lady, that's good."

And as for the Williamsburg hipsters, whose messages are expressed in pop culture references just as surely as they are immortalized on fliers, some might say the moral is that getting older is like skateboarding: it is not a crime. Others might just say we built this city on rock 'n' roll.

— *New York Times*, August 21, 2004

TRacing Steps of the Man
Who Walked Away

I t has always seemed right to refer to Brick by his last name. I identify him by his trilby hats and aviator shades, his white T-shirts, his vests, his cool lean against the wooden frame of a screen-house door in Georgia. But I really got to understand Brick, and to call him that, by communing over email the past five years about freelance writing. Brick has come to be something like my spirit animal in that regard. Whether untangling the mystery of a particular editor; or reading each other's pitches; discussing openly the darker inclinations of holding a professional grudge; reveling in the victory of one of us being published in print; acknowledging and supporting the type of ambition that drives both of us to keep trying.

Before I actually knew him, Brick was perhaps the most ambitious writer at The New York Times, turning mundane newspaper assignments into something like the songs he grew up writing; into the art collected in this book. You are an artist, Brick says, and it is true of him, and I live by those words. Brick, who can take a story about the summer and evoke its textures of soggy coasters and carnival light; a story about the Arena Football League and distill in one sentence the melancholy of aging, of failing, of never living up to maybe what you wanted; and a story, the next story, that I can't imagine anyone else writing, about a guy named Jimmy Moy, whose mere footsteps Brick found the lyrics in, a story about a guy who one day had to walk away.

—Justin Heckert

DATELINE: Park Slope, Brooklyn

He walked these avenues and then he was gone, as the inhabitants of one city give way to the next, as some are hurried along. Everyone leaves behind a name, a time, a place and a role, and his were Jimmy Moy, 1960, Park Slope, Brooklyn: the man who never returned.

A cataclysm's sudden vacancy leaves the memory of the disappeared, and the great imponderables visited upon the ancient Mayans, the Lost Colony in North Carolina, New Orleans, the long list. Where did they go, and will they come back, and why or why not, and what did they find? On the morning fire rained from the sky, Jimmy Moy left Brooklyn and a legend began.

"The people who lived here then," said Everett Ortner, who moved into one of the majestic brownstones that define this place three years after Jimmy Moy went away, "are all dead or moved out or sold out."

The legend started in a laundry, an immigrant business like countless others across the weary boroughs. Then as now, a man behind a counter could be a neighborhood figure, familiar face and passing acquaintance.

"He lived across the street," said Pauline McCaddin, whose family owned a funeral home on Seventh Avenue. "It was on the second floor of a brownstone, grocery underneath."

By the same coin, a man behind a counter could be a nonentity, ghost of a half-block's walk.

"I didn't go to the Chinese place," said Robert M. Nevin, who in 1960 lived at 126 Sterling Place, around the corner from the laundry. "I used a different tailor."

For Chon Quey Moy, the shop was a foothold in the city, sustenance and identity, a place in the world situated between Prospect Park and Flatbush Avenue rumbling on toward Midwood and Flatlands and the whole wide ocean.

In the 1959 Brooklyn telephone directory, behind a stately cover portrait of the library at Grand Army Plaza, Mr. Moy listed his home number, MAin 2-1446, at the shop's address, 26 Seventh Avenue. There he was on the page below Elsie Moxter from Shore Parkway.

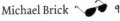

To Mr. Moy's contemporaries, he was the Chinese laundry-man of Park Slope. He cleaned shirts and folded them and returned them to their owners, and their owners were his neighbors, and his neighbors called him Jimmy. Park Slope was not the latter-day place of jogging strollers and purebred puppies. Houses on the park were offered for less than $30,000, though few banks would lend money to buy them.

"The neighborhood was in trouble," said Joseph Ferris, a retired teacher and state legislator. "Urban renewal was the poison pill they were offering for the abandoned buildings. This was the nadir."

Friday, Dec. 16, 1960, 10 a.m.: A wet snow was falling from clouds gathering low over Seventh Avenue. Slush in the streets. Harry Harrison spinning Chubby Checker on the radio, Christmas shopping. Drip coffee, subway tokens, morning. Mrs. Robert Nevin standing there in front of the dresser in a bathrobe, her babies asleep. Same day, 11 a.m.: A DC-8 jetliner collides with a Super Constellation over Staten Island and the wreckage burns in the Park Slope streets. A woman is trapped in a burning car. The Pillar of Fire Church burns, and bedrooms and storefronts burn, and the streets seem to be burning, and 135 would be the number of the dead.

The next morning the papers called it the worst aviation disaster of all time.

Dostoyevsky once said there are but two books written: A man goes on a journey and a stranger comes to town. To that end, the New York newspapers found Stephen Baltz, 11, the lone survivor aboard the DC-8. He was photographed dazed and scared under a passer-by's umbrella in the snow, a living symbol of hope to frame the horror for posterity, but he lived only a day.

The editors of *The New York Herald Tribune* wrote of Stephen, "And when he, too, died 24 hours later, the final grim sentence was written — and written in such a way as to concentrate all the horror and heartbreak of the story."

Fools believe in final sentences. The day fire fell from the sky was not to disappear from memory, but when Stephen died the chroniclers of Brooklyn's heartache needed a new protagonist. It happened that a man named Moy had been running a laundry shop at 73 degrees 58 minutes 25 seconds west longitude, 40 degrees 40 minutes 37 seconds north latitude, the corner of Seventh Avenue and Sterling Place. And now he was gone.

"What has happened since to Sterling Place?" asked an article in *The New York Times* four months after the crash. "To Jimmy Moy, the Chinese laundryman who vanished shortly after the crash, leaving the lights burning and neatly packaged shirts on the shelves of his seared shop?"

The writer answered her own question, finding Mr. Moy in Manhattan looking for another laundry job, and quoted him as saying, "I'm 70 years old and I don't feel good." How he felt was more detail than the legend required. Jimmy Moy quit Park Slope for Manhattan, left his business and his home, and that act alone would serve to evoke the day the plane fell to earth in Brooklyn.

Forty-three years later, a magazine called the *Park Slope Reader* would revisit the crash and mention "Jimmy Moy, who owned a laundry on the parlor floor at 26 Seventh Avenue, decided to move to Manhattan."

The man who never returned is a common legend, said Steve Zeitlin, executive director of City Lore, because it describes two ways of navigating life and times. In one way, Mr. Zeitlin said, people "want to come back to the places they once lived; the other being a very American way of wanting to invent yourself from scratch."

"When somebody walks away and never comes back," he said, "they're in some ways doing a disservice to the community they leave behind, even if they try to find a new life for themselves."

The new life Chon Quey Moy found in his 70's flashes past in five editions of the Manhattan telephone directory. There he is on East Eighth Street through 1962, then on First Avenue near 82nd Street through 1968. By 1970, his name is gone from the Manhattan directory.

A final accounting appears in a thick black volume marked Deaths and Fetal Deaths Recorded in 1974, City of New York. There, Medical Examiner Case No. 6,532 is described as Moy, Chon. The type is small and the names are dozens to a page, but the space under Boro is marked K, for county of Kings.

The certificate on file in the Municipal Archives shows that on Oct. 14, 1974, a death was reported in apartment 4R at 560 Lincoln Place. The address is in Crown Heights, not Park Slope but Brooklyn just the same. The man who left the world that day had a wife and a son, and he was first identified as James Moy. On the certificate, someone added Chon Quey, formal nomenclature.

But the language of bookkeeping leaves no room for intimacies or nicknames, for neighbors or blocks, for things everybody saw, for airplanes falling out of the sky. The pages do not explain that this vessel, brought down by coronary artery disease after 84 years, was the body of Jimmy the Chinese laundryman, the man who never did return.

—*The New York Times*, November 18, 2005

Dusk of the Drummer

I once heard someone say that every sentence should be the act of earning the reader's commitment to the next sentence. Topspin, it's called. I've been envious of Michael Brick's topspin since I first noticed his byline in The New York Times more than a decade back. Some of his stories, like the 459-word "Shaken and Stirred" column below, made me feel like I was rolling down some glorious hill.

Reading Brick, for me, is the repetitive act of asking: How the hell do you do that? I still wonder that about the following tone poem.

A few years ago, Brick was kind enough to help me as I put a book proposal together. He shared his proposal for "Saving the School," and let on that he was shocked by how much of the proposal was necessarily centered on selling the book.

Long into the process, he told his agent, "Soon we'll be done with the selling, and I can really concentrate on the writing."

"They're the same thing," she said.

"She's right," he told me. "We're selling the next word, every time."

—Ben Montgomery

DATELINE: Brooklyn, New York

The showman wears suspenders and a red-trimmed cummerbund, an insurance policy for pants. His pleated shirt is ornamented with black studs and red bow tie, his pinkie with a silver ring. He smells like baby powder, and he spits when he talks and wipes his mouth with paper napkins, and he jabs at the air. He looks made out of old tires and paste.

His stage is a glass-walled barroom in Sunset Park in south Brooklyn, with lights done up for Christmas, dim chandeliers like Superman's Fortress of Solitude and the television always on. He claims an audience of lawyers and doctors, magazine editors and titans of record companies, great favorites all.

The showman gives his full name as Peter Carmine Gaetano Napolitano, and he speaks of stages seen, bandstands of a bygone New York, disco halls and late, late nights and platinum records on other men's walls. The telephone rings, and he answers:

"Good evening. You've reached Melody Lanes. How may we help you? Yes, this is the bowling place."

When he hangs up, the show will start again for the unwatching eyes of the lane matron, the football fan and the bowler waiting for a bucket of beer. All the tribes of Brooklyn segregate themselves lanewise, skullcaps from ball caps, high-tops from combat boots. The loudspeaker plays Lisa Lisa & Cult Jam, and the bowlers drink and squint hard and say junior high seems unimproved this time around.

The showman announces he has cured writer's block and the shakes, has a head full of invented phrases dictionary-bound. His patter is riled stream of consciousness and runs in figure eights.

"I don't like motivational speakers, though they say I could do that," he says. "They're talking to a group of successful people who are answering as a unit. Why would a successful person want to be in a place like that?"

A sign on the bar advertises Pete's Special, "It's Green." Every bottle in reach contributes to the mixture, but its inventor will not partake.

"It knocks me out," Mr. Napolitano says.

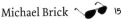

Then the shots are gone, and 2 o'clock is gone, and the last customers are gone in outsize camouflage, cockeyed caps and big jeans and no belts. The showman takes out a duffel bag, and there are pictures of square sunglasses and leisure suits, chest hair and Pete on drums. Bearded Pete and his girl camera-ready before brown wallpaper long out of fashion.

"When I croak, I have this bag," the showman says. "I'm not alone. I'm not afraid. When you're yourself, you say, 'I did what I had to do.'"

PETE'S SPECIAL
Adapted from Melody Lanes

> 1 1/2 ounces Alize
> 1 1/2 ounces Wild Turkey
> 1 1/2 ounces Bacardi 151
> 1 1/2 ounces Malibu coconut rum
> 1 1/2 ounces pineapple juice
> Dash blue Curacao
> Pour ingredients in order over ice. Shake, strain, pour shots

—*The New York Times*, January 22, 2006

New Orleans Arena League Team Casting Quite a Spell

Brick's written a lot about dreams and time. Elsewhere in this collection is an injured, aging hockey goalie from the Canadian plains still striving in the suburbs of Texas, the outcome inevitable, the destination unknown. There's a drummer with white hair and a small, full duffel, tales of "stages seen." "I'm not alone. I'm not afraid," the man says, and Brick hears him. Read about Ruby's, and the bar's not a bar; it's "an airy gap," where the days pass but the clock stops. "I'm glad for what I've got," one of the patrons says, "glad when the sun comes out," "glad to see the moon and stars," and Brick hears her, too. And here we meet a fading player in a last-chance league, a quarterback for a team called the VooDoo, who keeps old championship rings in a dresser drawer in the house where he lives with his parents, who chases the life he longs for in an arena called The Graveyard, who runs onto the field through what Brick describes as "an elaborate cemetery set," who wants so badly to stand in the light for as long as it lasts. In hope there is risk, and Brick knew it. He made music before he made stories, and so maybe that's why. Maybe that's why his voice, all and only his, is this unmistakable mixture of audacity and humility, discernment and mercy. It stands as a reminder for the reader ready to receive such a message from between the inky sentences of a metropolitan broadsheet, and to carry it out and into the rest of our unjust world.

—Michael Kruse

DATELINE: New Orleans

At 26, Danny Wimprine lives with his parents, not far from his old high school, in a room full of timeworn football posters and state championship rings. His father has a dog named Boots, and Boots likes chasing squirrels. Sometimes Boots will catch a squirrel and eat it, and other times the squirrel will get away.

Last Wednesday afternoon, there was a righteous chase, but the squirrel reached the chain-link fence ahead of Boots. So Wimprine followed along and laughed and told Boots she was a good girl just for keeping at it, then loped off at a pace suggesting he had all day.

Wimprine knew something about not getting what you want, but for the moment he seemed at ease, savoring his new role as the hometown hero of the off-season, quarterback of the New Orleans VooDoo, aspiring champions of the Arena Football League.

"The other night we went to get an ice cream, and a lady and her daughter, every time they thought you weren't looking, they'd look over," said Wimprine's father, Ronnie.

By the standards of arena football, even star players count themselves lucky to receive a look over ice cream. But the VooDoo, 7-2 and in first place in the Southern Division, has been charmed. After a season lost to Hurricanes Katrina and Rita, the team has enjoyed the embrace of this damaged city, where many people still sleep in tents under highway overpasses.

The VooDoo has sold 13,000 season tickets for the spring, a record for the league. Its home games regularly sell out, though actual attendance has fallen more than a thousand short of capacity at the 16,021-seat New Orleans Arena. Seizing on the popularity, the league has scheduled its championship game here for the second year running, on July 27.

"It's all the young kids — young, young, young," said Blanca Maya, a taxi driver who keeps an amulet to ward off the evil eye dangling from her rearview mirror. "They go crazy."

Wearing black and purple uniforms adorned with images of a skull in a top hat, the team seeks to evoke the New Orleans of the

Widow Paris, gris-gris and dark Sunday nights on Decatur Street. Its cheerleaders call themselves the VooDoo Dolls. Its fans call the arena the Graveyard.

"They love a great show, and they love to dress up," said Rita Benson LeBlanc, whose family owns the team. "They're very creative. It's costume night every time we have a game."

In a city that took its time rallying around the Hornets of the N.B.A. on their dazzling run to the playoffs, the groundswell for arena football has arrived in unpredicted fashion. The $8 ticket price provides a partial explanation. And Louisiana is football country.

But the VooDoo, formed as an expansion team with open tryouts in 2003, also started out with the advantage of resources from the Benson family, owners of the Saints. Only the Dallas and Atlanta arena franchises share such intimate ties to the N.F.L.

At the Saints' headquarters, the VooDoo has its own locker room and offices, plus the support of Saints coaches, operations staff and equipment managers. From the first season, the team's sales agents have made calls to Saints season-ticket holders, said Marcus J. Boyle, director of special events for the organization.

The VooDoo players practice inside a cavernous hangar on artificial turf lined with the hash marks of a full-size field. To simulate the boiling pot of arena football, coaching assistants block off a smaller field with four-foot-high inflatable walls. Mindful of the N.F.L. coaches wandering around, the VooDoo players work out with vigor, whooping, clapping and diving over the walls.

"Come on, let's go, pay attention to the ball!" Wimprine said to his teammates during practice last Wednesday.

In the fast-paced passing game of arena football, where field goals are considered defensive stops and running the ball is practically a trick play, quarterbacks are even more central figures than their N.F.L. counterparts. The VooDoo coaches found theirs living a mile or so behind their practice facility.

Wimprine had led John Curtis Christian School to consecutive state championships and broken just about every passing record the University of Memphis could offer before failing to secure a job in the N.F.L.

"When you don't go to a big school and you're only 6 feet tall, sometimes you don't get as many chances," Wimprine said last week as he drove home from practice.

The VooDoo coach, Mike Neu, approached Wimprine in 2006, while he was selling earthmovers down the road at Scott Equipment. Wimprine had been at the job only five months, selling one backhoe and one excavator, but the potential commission exceeded $100,000 a year in a city still digging out from floodwaters. The Voodoo offered him $27,000.

For 2007, Wimprine signed on as the third-string quarterback. Ascending to starter by trades and injuries this season, he has won his first five games and lost only once, on the road against Dallas.

With his schoolboy haircut, easy smile and handy prayer book, Wimprine has found no shortage of admirers here. He says yes ma'am, quotes his father and coddles the puppy adopted by his girlfriend of 11 years. Between practices, his schedule last week included visiting a Kiwanis Club at 7 a.m. on Thursday.

Later that afternoon, Wimprine and two teammates played bingo with children in a pediatric ward and signed autographs for cancer patients. In a chemotherapy suite, Wimprine gave Clyde and Joyce Barrois game tickets.

"I'm aware that they do a lot of good," Joyce said as Wimprine walked away. "You see them on TV. They're good for New Orleans."

On Friday night, the VooDoo hosted winless Utah. Outside the arena, children jumped in an inflatable trampoline, mascots in skeleton costumes walked on stilts, a band covered Def Leppard and balloon-animal makers did their thing.

"We just love New Orleans and what it stands for," said Linda Poillion, a season-ticket holder who had driven from Hammond, La., for the game. "It's just a lot of fun; it's real family-oriented."

The Voodoo took the field through the gates of an elaborate cemetery set, with pyrotechnics blasting over the mausoleums. Banners advertised businesses that could hardly afford N.F.L. sponsorship.

The whole show catered to momentary attention spans. An announcer kept yelling about the VooDoo defense. The cheerleaders

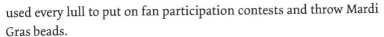

used every lull to put on fan participation contests and throw Mardi Gras beads.

On the narrow field, Wimprine was not much of a scrambler. For most plays, he just dropped back and waited to throw the ball or get knocked down, sometimes both. To begin the second quarter, he threw a touchdown pass nearly the length of the 50-yard field while getting clobbered. The crowd ate it up.

After halftime, Wimprine threw another long touchdown pass. Then the VooDoo forced a fumble, and he threw a short one. Then the Blaze failed to recover an onside kick. Cue Wimprine, touchdown, cheerleaders, beads.

When time ran out, the VooDoo had won, 70-56, on the strength of nine touchdown passes. Children swarmed the field for a half-hour autograph session mandated by the league. A long line formed around Wimprine, who stood under a goal post signing helmets, noisemakers, shirts, caps and footballs. A girl with a camera told him to say cheese.

"Cheese," Wimprine said, smiling under the bright lights in the end zone, in no hurry to drive back to his father's house, where Boots patrolled the backyard and all those old championship rings were stuffed in a dresser drawer.

—*The New York Times*, April 29, 2008

Jingo Unchained

Disclaimer: I met the author of this story once, spent a writerly weekend with him drinking beer, banging on musical instruments, croaking oldies and trying to figure out how to write magazine stories wonderfully well. He gave off the impression that he wasn't sure how to do that and had to find out, even on the hour ride to the airport that I was lucky enough to provide him when it was time for everyone to stagger home. It was only later, when I started reading his stuff, that I discovered that couldn't possibly be true.

The story of his that you're about to read is a prime example of a writer refusing to be suckered into the obvious. Walking into a pro wrestling arena full of cartoonish characters, resisting the chance to let fly with overhead chops and flying dropkicks, conveying a deeper reality instead with deft nods and nudges.

The opening paragraph posits the story's theme—the fluidity and exploitation of identity in America—without ever quite declaring itself, like a five-spot left on a park bench. Then we're escorted further and further into those shadows without once feeling the author's hand on our neck.

At the end, we're left with the sinking feeling that we're reading a story not about American pro wrestlers... but about American politicians. That's the payoff of a story built by Brick, but delivered by feather.

—Gary Smith

The spit of land at the mouth of the Nueces River defied five settlement parties before 1839, when a Yankee speculator, Colonel Henry Lawrence Kinney, demonstrated the benefits of illegal trade across the new border separating Texas from Mexico. The colonel, who'd awarded himself that rank for unspecified actions performed in Florida's Seminole Wars, would go on to pursue a colorful career that included charges of treason and election to the Texas congress before he died in a gunfight in Matamoros. Despite the intercession of a devastating hurricane in 1919, Kinney's Nueces outpost grew to become present-day Corpus Christi, a city of 307,953 with such tourist attractions as an aquarium, a decommissioned aircraft carrier, and the Mirador de la Flor, a monument to the Tejano pop singer Selena whose inscription reads, in part, HER PERSONA ENRICHED THE LIVES OF THOSE SHE TOUCHED. There's also a minor-league ballpark, where one night two summers ago I saw a white man taunt a largely Mexican crowd to the edge of violence.

I arrived at Whataburger Field in the high heat of an early-September afternoon and was met at the gate by a man named Steven Ship. Ship is a ponytailed music-industry veteran turned TV producer turned fight promoter who has spent years trying to bring big-time Mexican wrestling—*lucha libre*—to the United States. He'd called a few weeks earlier to say that he'd landed a slot on two MTV channels and that there was a new fighter he wanted me to see.

"My name is RJ Brewer, and I'm from the greatest city in the United States: Phoenix, Arizona," the fighter said in a video that Ship sent me.

> I never had to scale a fence to get what I wanted. I cut lawns because I wanted to, not because I had to. See, my mother is a very, very powerful woman, probably the most powerful woman in the United States of America. And she taught me at an early age that if I see something wrong, make it right. That's exactly what she's doing in Phoenix, Arizona, and that's exactly what I'm going to do here.

Ship's fighter was the make-believe son of Arizona governor Jan Brewer, famous for both her aggressive anti-immigration policies and her finger-wagging confrontation with President Obama beside Air Force One on a Phoenix tarmac. In 2010, Brewer signed into law Arizona Senate Bill 1070, which allows state authorities to direct police to check the immigration status of persons detained in stops. While opponents call it an invitation to racial profiling, the law survived a U.S. Supreme Court challenge with its central provision intact and has inspired similar legislation throughout the country. Attaching his fighter to Brewer and her law was a canny move on Ship's part, meant to get the maximum possible rise out of his audience, which is at least 80 percent Mexican-American.

Putting over a pro-wrestling persona is not easy. The task requires a thorough mastery of "kayfabe," a carny-derived term for the extreme strain of method acting peculiar to the sport. American pro wrestlers treat kayfabe with a devotion that requires denying the obvious. It's a head game. When you know you're faking and the audience knows you're faking and you know the audience knows you know you're faking because the fact that *pro wrestling is fake* has been documented, verified, and repeated to the point of cliché, and yet you stay in character on the walk from the locker room to your Mazda just in case someone is pointing his phone's camera at you from a window above the alley — that's kayfabe.

Luchadores elevate kayfabe to the realm of the soul. They wear artful costumes designed to telegraph their allegiances, though their audiences fully expect those allegiances to shift, prove false, and suffer betrayals for reasons that may never be explained.

* * *

Ship led me to the locker room. We were accompanied by the stage manager, who was predicting a riot. "My job," he said, "is to get him out of the building alive tonight." Then I stood before him: the bad man of *lucha libre*, dressed in cargo shorts, a muscle shirt, and sneakers, sitting on a weight bench owned by a Double-A affiliate of the Houston Astros. He had a seven-dollar haircut and an attentive gaze.

"I see the kids screaming at me, I see the middle fingers, and I say to myself, They don't belong here. They don't have the right to be screaming at me. They're probably not even here legally," he said. "I don't try to be the RJ Brewer character; at that point I *am*. It's like selling cars or being a waiter or bartender at a restaurant. You're on-stage. You're just selling a different product. I'm selling my views. I'm selling hate."

During the interview, "RJ" did something I wasn't expecting: he indicated my notebook, looked me in the eye, and disavowed some of his character's more extreme beliefs. This presented a major breach of kayfabe, one so startlingly flagrant as to seem calculated. In fact, admitting the obvious point that he wasn't actually related to Brewer while insisting "My message is real" may simply have added another level to the performance. While we were at it, he confirmed that his real name was John Stagikas, that he was thirty-one, and that he was from Framingham, Massachusetts. He'd played wide receiver for Assumption College in Worcester until surgery to remove a cyst in his throat derailed him in his junior year. In 2000, having lost what he called "the football bug," he'd enrolled in wrestling classes under the tutelage of the famous Killer Kowalski.

"Make the people notice you," Kowalski advised him.

At this Stagikas had failed consistently. He chose the hope-lessly earnest stage name "Hurricane" John Walters, finishing off opponents with a combination backbreaker rack and facedown slam he called the Hurricane DDT. Barrel-chested and athletic, he carried on as though endowed with some innate righteousness for which he deserved to win. His all-American-golden-boy posture was easy to lampoon. He was playing the traditional "face," a role out of fashion since the prime of Hulk Hogan, whom the Hurricane by comparison made seem a subtle master of character development. In the early aughts, a period known to wrestling's followers as the Attitude Era, Stagikas/Walters was a man out of time. For most of the next decade, he shuttled between circuits of varying repute. In the process, he learned that technical proficiency is a surprisingly small part of the business. What he was doing was less *pro* wrestling than just very good wrestling. Nobody wanted to see that.

His career might have ended right there—with lightning-striped tights in the back of his closet and a set of Google results to explain to potential employers—except that Steve Ship came around looking for a new white star to round out an impressive cast of *técnicos* (*lucha libre*'s equivalent of the American "face"), *rudos* (antagonists, who in America are called "heels"), *minis* (self-explanatory), and cross-dressing performers known as *exóticos*.

In John Stagikas, Ship saw his ideal RJ Brewer. He didn't need to tinker much with his Walters persona; he just needed to give it a different context. Ship planned to turn all of Stagikas's failings into strengths, transforming him from unimaginative face into clown prince of the *rudos*, and to build a North American franchise—English-language crossover matches, action figures, video games—around his gringo buffoonery.

* * *

Steve Ship is not the first promoter to put a nationalistic provocateur in the ring. His inspiration derives from the wrestlers billed as Nikolai Volkoff of the Soviet Union and the Iron Sheik of Iran, who enjoyed long careers during wrestling's Reagan-era heyday. Making the same concept work in *lucha libre* has been a matter of escalating the rhetoric, finding the right performer, and understanding who the real heel is. Several years ago, at Arco Arena in Sacramento, Ship introduced me to a twenty-six-year-old by the name of Jack Evans, a compact, rheumy-eyed chain-smoker with a permanent hangover and a fade haircut. Cast as a leader of the Foreign Legion, a horde of non-Mexican wrestlers, Evans would pester the crowd with racial meanness until the native *luchador* Super Fly and his partner, Crazy Boy, who wore a red basketball jersey that said MEXICAN POWER, came out to crush him. This was all back before Governor Brewer signed SB 1070, so Jack Evans was just supposed to be a typical American jerk.

I'd been hanging around backstage on the 2009 Invasion Tour, an American offshoot of the Mexican Asistencia Asesoría y Administración league, for a newspaper series on outsider sports, the kind that tend to be televised only on channels entirely devoted to televising them. For several years, the AAA had been falling behind its chief rival in Mexico, the Consejo Mundial de Lucha Libre, and hoped to make up ground north of the border. A *luchador* called Abismo Negro, who was supposed to join us on Ship's Invasion Tour, had just died of a heart attack. But some pretty big stars — La Parka and El Mesías in particular — plus the usual cast of *minis* and *exóticos* did come on board.

Back in the locker room, I watched a Canadian veteran named Vampiro ice his neck while a *luchador* called Konnan sat on the rubdown table. There was a buffet spread with *queso blanco*, pickled jalapeños, and mango juice.

"I swear to God, when I hit that railing, I thought I broke my fucking leg," Vampiro said. "And then when you hit me in the back of the neck..."

"My bad," Konnan said. "It won't happen again."

Vampiro gave that some consideration. The *luchadores* were in their forties, and they had been hitting and kicking and body-slamming one another for many years. No matter what Konnan said, it would almost certainly happen again.

"For a couple guys who are already broken-down," Vampiro said, "we can really light it up."

Konnan agreed that they could really light it up. Their fight had drawn nearly 6,000 spectators, despite Vampiro's less-than-wholehearted commitment to the entire undertaking. In a sport defined by elaborate masquerade, he left the locker room in sweats. Yet the crowd received him rapturously. As his business with Konnan wrapped up, I asked Vampiro how he'd gotten his start. He told me about growing up in Thunder Bay, Ontario. Born Ian Hodgkinson, he'd abandoned junior-league hockey for rock music and drugged his way through the L.A. goth scene of the late 1980s, compiling a résumé loaded with such superbly unverifiable gigs as Milli Vanilli bodyguard. By the early 1990s, still dressed in thick makeup, cowboy boots, and sprayed-out purple hair, he had turned up in Mexico City. Calling himself El Vampiro Canadiense, he painted his face whiter than its natural pallor. He draped long, dark braids over his eyes. With goth intensity, he entered the ring to Guns N' Roses's "Welcome to the Jungle." Cast against the traditional acrobatics and sexual slapstick of the sport, he was a glam-rock apostle of the north, a dark, brooding, and vagabond antihero.

His timing was magnificent. In a decade when NAFTA remade the continental economy, when the number of Mexicans living in the United States increased by 50 percent, to 20 million, and annual remittances nearly doubled, to $7 billion, Hodgkinson became a star of films (*Vampiro: Guerrero de la Noche*), a subject of corridos, and an object of lust. There were dolls and lunch boxes, posters and calendars. An advice column appeared under his name. *Circo* magazine named him one of the fifty most beautiful people in Latin America. Along the way, he traded Guns N' Roses for AC/DC's "Back in Black." His renown expanded no matter the inconsistency of his stage name: The Canadian Vampire Casanova, Vampiro Casanova, El Vampiro, or simply Vampiro. (When asked about these changes, Hodgkinson said, "I didn't speak fucking Spanish.") In *lucha libre,* as in politics, popular success flows from the astute selection of enemies, and Hodgkinson found an able foil in Charles Ashenoff, the bulky Cuban who wrestled as Konnan. Fueled by a fight over Vampiro's signature hairstyle, the two men began a feud they nurtured across decades.

"Vampiro, what can I say?" Konnan told *Pro Wrestling Torch* in 1994.

> He came into Mexico and he was a real big, big, big star. His popularity has dipped because a lot of times for press conferences he hasn't shown up, a lot of times he was gonna give away tickets at the Arena Mexico and he never showed up. Then he said he was going to quit wrestling because he had epilepsy and asthma, but yet he was going to start a rock band. I would publicly put in newspapers that it takes the same energy to play a guitar and jump up and down on stage as it does wrestling, so he can't have epilepsy or asthma. Then when his rock and roll career died, he came back into wrestling.

Though intended as trash talk, Konnan's account was fairly accurate: Hodgkinson had briefly quit wrestling to front a punk band, just because that was his thing. In light of his marginal grappling skills, manifest distractibility, and apparent disdain for the wrestling business, promoters started casting him as a *rudo*. But to fans on both sides of the border he remained a singularly enduring *técnico*. In 2005, he accepted a commission to lead a Mexico City chapter of the Guardian Angels vigilante group. Decades past his prime, Hodgkinson was doing this tour to "get the fuck out of Mexico City," he said, "and to shop." He was a hard man to know.

The morning after the Sacramento fight, he took a seat behind the bus driver, stretched out his bum leg, and began eating his breakfast of beef jerky and Milk Duds. The production coordinator was taking attendance—"Super Fly *está*, Laredo *está*"—and the driver was taking votes for the day's lunch stop. Mall food court beat out IHOP by a wide margin. As the bus rolled down I-80, the *luchadores* watched *Kung Fu Panda*.

At the Westfield mall in San Jose, the *luchadores* passed up a make-your-own-salad place and Hot Dog on a Stick, opting instead for Mongolian barbecue; then they did some shopping. They returned to the bus with tubs of protein powder from GNC and pink bags from Victoria's Secret. We all sat outside the bus and watched Jack Evans smoke some cigarettes and listened to him talk about the relative merits of the strip clubs in Mexico City versus here until the promoters called *vámonos*. We drove on to the Sheraton, then the arena.

When the lights dimmed that night, Jack Evans, Silver King, and the rest of the Foreign Legion got the crowd worked up. The heroic *técnicos* took their scripted beating. Then a hush fell. And just when all seemed lost, that familiar crunch of electric guitar erupted from the speakers, that bear hug of a bass line, that nails-to-chalkboard screech:

> Back in black
> I hit the sack
> I been too long, I'm glad to be back

And here was Vampiro in black jeans, black armbands, and a black sleeveless shirt, a dark and ageless blur lurching down the runway,

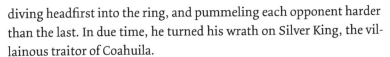

diving headfirst into the ring, and pummeling each opponent harder than the last. In due time, he turned his wrath on Silver King, the villainous traitor of Coahuila.

As the crowd urged him on, Vampiro lumbered around the ring, moved into the stands, then stopped to rest, his hands on his knees, at which point Silver King smashed him with a chair. The referee got in some blows, too. The assault went on and on, but never did the crowd lose faith. A chant went up: "Vam-pee-RO! Vam-pee-RO!"

Finally the great champion summoned the strength to flip Silver King onto the cement. He gave the crowd a slow burn. Bending to one knee, he reached down for the discarded chair as if it were the Sword in the Stone.

Soon enough Silver King would be vanquished, the damnable referee would get his, and the unmoored Canadian who fought for the Mexican cause would take his victory lap through a crowd clamoring with cries of *"Te quiero mucho"* to touch his dark and ragged garments. But as he raised the chair above his head in agonizing slow motion, taking up the weapon of desperados in the name of righteousness, Vampiro looked stricken, torn, hurt on some cosmic level, as if the whole continent were turning faithless and cruel and there was no way to tell what anybody might do next.

* * *

In preparation for my trip to Corpus Christi, I looked into how things had turned out for Vampiro. Under his real name, he was still listed as the leader of the Mexico City Guardian Angels. I also found a dispatch from the U.K. *Sun* that told how he'd slept through a burglary at his Guadalajara apartment, panicked at the sight of responding police officers, and leaped from his fourth-story bedroom window, breaking his back. When I contacted him to verify that account, he denied it, adding, "I don't have any interest at all in wrestling. I am out of touch and I just don't want to know about it anymore."

In Vampiro's absence, Ship had assembled a new cast with crossover appeal in mind. Some of his masked *técnicos* billed their hometowns as Mexican cities—Guadalajara, Chihuahua, Torreón— but others claimed San Juan and even Atlanta. (Promotional materials noted that Marco Corleone, a spiky-haired gringo, had paid his dues in Mexico, "dominating the ring and capturing his audience with the highest vertical leap in the business.")

About an hour before showtime, I stood under a giant statue of a home-run slugger, watching hundreds of Latino families pass through the gates of Whataburger Field. There were thumb-wrestling puppets and face painters for the kids. Vendors hawked *máscaras*. Ring girls posed in flag bikinis—both Mexican and American. A man dressed up as a taco distributed T-shirts via slingshot.

I wandered down under the bleachers to watch the *luchadores* make their preparations and to find the promotion's lead writer, Alex Abrahantes. He'd wrestled on the American circuit as Too Phat Yutzak Arafat, Keeper of the Harem, after a trainer told him, "You look dark. I'm going to make you an Arab." Abrahantes's path from there to inventing characters like RJ Brewer wasn't tough to imagine. I asked what kind of wrestler it would take to bring the act to life.

"When you walk into the crowd," Abrahantes said, "you have this energy where you evoke emotion from them and you draw energy from them." He explained that Stagikas "has done a great job of portraying the character and making it his own. He'll add things to the character. He has a really good mind for psychology, which is a big part of this industry."

As Abrahantes spoke, I considered the suggestion that a few script changes might elevate John Stagikas/Hurricane Walters/RJ Brewer from a strained Captain America act into a credibly venomous xenophobe, just like that. Americans had loved booing Nikolai Volkoff and the Iron Sheik, but they seemed genuinely to despise Rowdy Roddy Piper, a Canadian who portrayed a Scotsman. Maybe there's just some ineffable quality, a kind of metakayfabe, that allows performers comfortable beyond a certain level of cognitive dissonance to cast a spell over their audience.

Across the locker room, Stagikas stood alone, shirtless; s.b. 1070 was emblazoned on the backside of his tights. I followed him out to the hall, where he rested his forehead against a fence near some disused pretzel machines. Deep in thought, perhaps, becoming RJ Brewer. He paced a tight circle, cracked his neck, and peeked out at the crowd. On the loudspeakers, an announcer asked whether Corpus Christi was ready. Brewer prepared to "cut a promo," provoking the crowd before returning to the locker room while the undercard is fought.

"One on each side, guys, let's go," the stage manager said. Uniformed police officers moved into position, flanking Brewer, who walked out across the turf with the swagger of a beach bully. "Meh-hee-CO! Meh-hee-CO!" people chanted. Then Brewer took the microphone.

"Finally I get to wrestle in a baseball park," he announced, "which means plenty of fresh air, which means I don't have to smell you people."

When he'd finished his introductory speech, he walked back toward third base and down into the dugout. He stood at the gateway to the tunnel leading back to the locker room, artificial fog obscuring his face. His police escorts started to giggle. Before he could slip completely out of view, he was confronted by a boy of perhaps six, who ran down the aisle and declared, in English: "Hey! I don't like you."

"I don't like you either, you little twerp," Brewer said. "Get out of my face."

Down the hall, the stage manager kept up the aggro patter — "My job isn't complete," he told Brewer, "until you get shanked in an alley somewhere" — though the crowd outside seemed more inclined to cheer for airborne *camisetas* than to shank anybody. When the *minis* and *exóticos* performed, rollicking laughter sounded in the night air, and when Mini Park led a dance-off, children selected from the audience won by acclamation.

* * *

Back in the locker room, Stagikas practiced a few moves with the *luchador* who was to vanquish him in the final act, Blue Demon Jr., then attempted small talk.

"How about just over the border, the Mexico–U.S. border? Is it hot there?" Stagikas inquired.

Blue Demon Jr. affirmed that climatological assessment. Stagikas walked the hall, presumably getting back into character. He did some push-ups, listened for his cue, then entered the ring as RJ Brewer.

The *luchadores* set to each other. A smack in the mouth, a rub of the jaw, and the crowd was chanting again, louder and sharper, "Meh-hee-CO! Meh-hee-CO!" Brewer complained to the ref, faked quitting the match, and then threw a sucker punch. By the time Brewer hoisted Blue Demon Jr. to the turnbuckle, unlaced his opponent's mask, and started to pry it off, grown men were leaning forward in their seats: for a *luchador*, no humiliation can surpass an unmasking.

Just as rehearsed, Blue Demon Jr. caught Brewer in the ribs. The violence went on and on, a trading of body slams and clotheslinings, great exclamations, groans and squeals, near-pin after near-pin until at last the figure of RJ Brewer lay prone on the mat, under the able grasp of the adopted son of Blue Demon, champion of Nuevo Leon. The people seemed pleased as they went off to buy more T-shirts and masks. Of course, they couldn't do much about the power people like Jan Brewer have in their adopted homeland, but that night they'd watched her putative son stumble away, holding his head in both hands, defeated, shamed, and perhaps something more.

Stagikas could not have known it then, but the next few years would bring stardom. He had managed to make himself noticed. The crowds would grow. The production would elevate him to the leadership of a *rudo* gang called the Right. In January, he appeared in character on *Nightline*, telling an interviewer, "this is really how I feel." Currently, Brewer and his gang are on a nine-city tour making stops in Houston, San Jose, Los Angeles, and, yes, Phoenix. So far as anyone knows, the American face Hurricane Walters has been permanently retired.

—*Harper's Magazine*, May 2013

Brisket Bandit exposes flaw: Justice system struggles to stop Repeat offenders

*S*itting in an East Austin coffee shop waiting to meet Michael Brick *for the first time, I had a pit in my stomach. I was a shy, 21-year-old kid who decided to study journalism because I liked writing in high school. And now I was about to interview for a job helping a* New York Times *reporter research a book about a local high school struggling to stay open another year. Basically, I was in over my head.*

Waiting to meet Michael that day, I didn't know he would become one of my greatest mentors.

In the middle of all the craziness leading up the publication of his first book, Michael took the time to buy me a barbecue sandwich and ask how my classes were going. He sent me job postings after I graduated. He read the stories I wrote for my first real reporting gig out of school. He did all of this while turning out some of the most beautiful, the most human stories you'll ever hope to read.

Since the first day I sat down for coffee with Michael, I learned a lot from him. Most of it has stuck with me through the years, and even through I'm not a reporter anymore, I still try to live by it:

—Be persistent.

—Pay attention to the little things. Details matter.

—Stay humble.

—Be interested in people. Care about them. Michael did this in spades.

He cared about Anabel Garza, and Candice Kaiser, and Derrick Davis, and all the other teachers and students from Reagan High that played a role in "Saving the School." He cared about James Cordell Avery, Austin's brisket bandit. Long after Avery's name stopped appearing in the food blogs, Michael wrote this compelling piece about how he had slipped through the cracks of the criminal justice system. And during his time as editorial adviser to the student newspaper at the University of Texas, Michael cared about all the students he mentored. I'm lucky to count myself as one of them.

—Lena Price

DATELINE: Austin, Texas

The man behind the glass partition was famous. His photograph appeared on statewide news sites and national food blogs, wanted as the architect of a brazen scheme.

When officials requested public assistance in his capture last year, they accused him of stealing thousands of dollars worth of meat from at least 19 grocery stores. He most likely devised an ad-hoc black market, police said, among the legitimate middlemen who connect ranchers to trendy steakhouses and barbecue pits.

His name is James Cordell Avery. Headline writers called him the Brisket Bandit.

In an interview at the Travis County Correctional Complex, Avery slurred through the telephone. He looked disheveled and sounded confused. He wore a hard glare, a thick beard and a striped jumpsuit.

"I didn't kill nobody, man," he said.

That may be true. Homicide is not among the many crimes ascribed to his name. At a time of high beef prices and boundless culinary obsession, though, his case actually drew far more attention than most murders.

Long after the food blogs have moved on, Avery lingers in the court system. His case underscores the challenges facing bipartisan lawmakers intent on reforming the criminal justice system.

For most of his life, Avery, 48, has been in and out of jail, caught in the revolving door of small-time busts, mental health exams and plea deals.

On a typical day, American jails hold 730,000 people, most convicted or simply accused of nonviolent crimes against property or public order, according to the Vera Institute of Justice, a nonpartisan research group.

Many people return time and again, unable to break the cycle. Some never get the help they need to treat drug addiction and mental illness. Some never take the help they get. Knowing the difference between the two is the enduring conundrum of policy makers.

"The system is failing to ask the very difficult but obvious question: Why does he keep doing this?" said Michele Deitch, a criminal justice policy expert at the University of Texas at Austin. "If all the system is doing is churning him out over and over again, why do we expect anything to change?"

The pattern is so typical for people accused of minor offenses, Deitch said, that "the jails even call them 'frequent fliers.'"

* * *

As a young man, Avery started compiling a record of convictions for joy riding, evading arrest and cocaine possession. He found trouble from here to San Patricio County. In 1990, a judge directed him toward a drug diversion program called "A Chance to Change."

Instead, Avery became a prolific shoplifter. Some people steal for thrills: the five-finger discount, sticking it to the man. Some steal things they need. Others steal things they want, with the act of stealing caught up in the desire.

The things Avery stole did not command lucrative prices on the black market. Some seemed almost worthless. Misdemeanor charges sent him to jail for 85 days in 2007 and 20 days in 2009. Each time, he was fined more than $200.

In July 2009, Home Depot employees trailed him as he loaded a cart with three weed-eaters. Pleading guilty, he was sentenced to 70 days in jail.

Four months later, he was arrested again. A loss-prevention agent at a Wal-Mart who was walking the floor "undercover," according to court documents, watched Avery swap his black T-shirt for a gray Longhorns T-shirt. The shirt cost $10. Avery also picked up two $60 sewing kits from the arts and crafts department. Though the total value amounted to only $130, he was charged with "enhanced" felony theft due to his previous convictions.

But in October 2009, Avery was found mentally incompetent to stand trial. He was committed to a state hospital for a process known as "competency restoration."

Department of State Health Services officials declined to discuss his case. In general, said Carrie Williams, a spokeswoman for the agency, the Incompetent to Stand Trial designation means a person lacks the ability to consult an attorney or understand legal proceedings. Last year, 2,066 people accused of crimes in Texas faced competency restoration, up from 2,035 in 2013 and 1,845 in 2012.

At the state hospital, Avery would be held until doctors judged him "to have a rational and factual understanding of the legal proceedings," Williams said. "This involves stabilization, psychological testing, medication, education about the proceedings and also some basic rehabilitation therapies, such as life skills."

Six months later, deemed fit to stand trial by state doctors, Avery pleaded guilty to stealing the T-shirt and sewing kits. He was sentenced to seven months in jail.

* * *

Over the years, Avery returned to court dozens of times, usually on theft charges. Listing no dependents and no income, he was represented by a different court-appointed lawyer nearly every time. Few responded to calls from a reporter to discuss his life; those who called back said they did not remember him at all.

As a shoplifter, his performance never improved much with practice. His behavior sometimes made people question his sanity.

In November 2011, for example, Avery was riding in the passenger seat of a Buick pulled over in connection with the theft of a television from Wal-Mart. According to a sworn statement from the arresting officer, he said, "I don't know what is going on," then ran across four lanes of traffic. Charged with evading arrest, he again was found incompetent to stand trial.

Back on the street, Avery hit the jewelry counters of pawn shops and discount stores. He took an unsophisticated approach: Ask to see a ring, then run away with it.

Once, police say, he took off with a 14-carat white gold band with a marquise diamond marked for sale at $789.99. He was arrested again, identified by a store clerk and sent for another mental examination. "Based on his likelihood to re-offend," prosecutors wrote in a court filing, "please consider awarding a high bond."

By 2014, Avery had become a familiar figure to law enforcement personnel. But they were not the only ones watching out for him. H-E-B Grocery Co., the San Antonio-based chain that operates more than 340 stores in Texas and Mexico, started documenting thefts of beef brisket by the cartload.

* * *

Brisket takes hours to smoke well. Beyond Texas barbecue joints and Jewish holiday feasts, the kosher cut from the chest of the cow has never achieved the popularity of the T-bone.

But demand rose sharply in recent years as restaurants of all kinds—from Fette Sau in New York to the fast-food chain Arby's—found inspiration in the methods of traditional pitmasters.

At the same time, supply dropped as droughts descended. Ranchers sent cattle to an early slaughter. Nationally, herd counts reached a 60-year low.

Last summer, wholesale brisket prices rose to more than $3 a pound, up from $2.03 the year before. Texas barbecue restaurants posted signs explaining price hikes. Some started running specials on chicken or pork ribs.

The prices tempted thieves. In the South Texas town of Alice, police arrested a man named Bobby Lee Gentry on charges of stealing two briskets. In San Antonio, three barbecue restaurants reported meat lost in burglaries. In the North Texas town of Denton, according to local news reports, a thief started a fire while grabbing a brisket directly off the smoker.

In May 2014, a man walked into an Austin H-E-B store that featured a wine steward, sushi bar and "Full-Service Meat Market offering USDA Prime, Natural and Organic Meats." According to police reports, a store employee watched the man load 10 briskets worth $421.41 into a cart. Confronted outside the store, the man ran away.

From surveillance footage at several stores, H-E-B loss prevention agents identified a pattern: While a Buick idled in the parking lot with a male driver, a tall man—and sometimes a woman acting as a lookout—would enter a store. The man would fill a cart with brisket, sometimes covering the merchandise with advertising fliers, and then walk out to the car.

In August 2014, the company distributed fliers to its employees, showing images of the man and woman, the getaway car and a cart full of brisket. The thefts continued. Sometimes, the man got away with the meat; sometimes employees scared him off.

* * *

Last fall, Austin police assigned Detective Rickey Jones, a military veteran with more than a decade of experience investigating theft, criminal mischief and assault cases. Interviewing H-E-B loss-prevention agents, Jones came away impressed. The thief "was stealing meat on an epic scale," he said. "Think about how many briskets you can get into a shopping cart. One basket alone was $900. That's a lot of meat."

Though he had surveillance footage and a license plate number from the getaway car—a golden 2002 sedan with a dented back quarter panel on the passenger side—Jones needed to identify the man in the video. He soon learned that investigators from other police departments were looking for the same thief.

A break came, Jones said, when a traffic stop produced Avery, who was wanted for theft at an H-E-B in a nearby suburb. In mid-October 2014, Avery served a 20-day jail sentence.

His booking photo gave investigators something to show witnesses. Avery has a shaved head and stands more than 6 feet tall, with recessed features and deep-set brown eyes. Several H-E-B employees recognized him.

Choosing four cases in which the meat was recovered, so he could assign an exact dollar value, Jones swore out a statement seeking authority to arrest Avery on charges of theft in excess of $2,000.

He also sought to identify a buyer. His thoughts drifted to 2011, when the city revoked licenses from a few restaurants accused of accepting stolen meat.

"What are you going to do with a whole basket of brisket?" he said. "Three is personal use, at most, I think."

On New Year's Eve, the Austin Police Department issued its request for help finding Avery. Locking on to the food angle, bloggers spread the word. Six days later, at 5:37 a.m., the Brisket Bandit came before a judge.

Case closed. Sort of.

* * *

Avery has not given up his accomplices or his buyers. From the perspective of law enforcement officials, Jones said, sending people to jail only to find them on the street committing the same crimes again can become "frustrating."

"What does it take to change the essence of a person?" Jones asked. "I can't answer that question."

Since January, Avery has been awaiting trial on charges of stealing the brisket and the rings from jewelry stores. In May, a prosecutor requested a mental health examination to determine his competency to stand trial.

No record of a result of the evaluation appears in his court file. The average length of stay for patients who have been restored to competency in felony cases is three months, according to the state Health Services Department.

The district attorney's office did not respond to interview requests. Neither did Avery's most recent lawyer, William Browning.

Gazing through the jailhouse partition, Avery leaned back in his chair. He said he hears demons. He said a visitor appeared to have power in his eyes. Asked the whereabouts of the stolen brisket, he mentioned men named Charlie and Bob, who "had power over me." He walked away from the phone, then came back. He denied any involvement in the thefts.

"I like chicken, man," Avery said. "I like chicken and pork chops."

Then the connection ended, and he returned to a familiar place.

—*The Houston Chronicle*, August 9, 2015

ARt oR vandalism?
A detective follows the tRail
of a gRaffiti aRtist
knoWn as "Kudos"

There are moments in all our lives so precious we not only visit them, but they visit us, popping into our heads seemingly out of nowhere. This is one of mine: Making Michael Brick laugh till he cried with my story of drunkenness, violence and poo.

Brick, a magnificent human being, is also a bit intimidating. I met him at a writing retreat called The Auburn Chautauqua, a magical place in the Georgia woods where we weird writers travel each fall to find our people. Brick is controlled, intense, confident. Talented as hell. Intellectually imposing. Physically imposing with his height and fedora-and-vest-wearing-coolness. If he wanted, he could wear sunglasses indoors (at night!), yet he's warm, sincerely listening to others, helping clear plates off the table, lovingly showing photos of his children.

He is the best of us.

But not silly. Or so I thought. It was 2010 and I covered the cops beat in Pasco County for the Tampa Bay Times. I didn't bring this story to the retreat to be reviewed and I can't remember how it came up, but it went like this: A 21-year-old named Justin Barker drank a shit-ton of caffeinated alcohol called Four Loko, took off his clothes and went on a naked rampage, breaking into homes, cutting himself, smearing blood everywhere, scaring an elderly woman in the street with his nudity. In one home, he ripped off an oven door and defecated in the living room and kitchen before passing out in another house and not remembering a thing.

The oven door is what nailed it for Brick. He convulsed with laughter, barely able to talk. How do you rip off an oven door? Why the oven and not some other appliance? Was it talking to him? "What did you say? Fuck you, Oven!" Soon we all were pretending to be that crazy drunk dude—arguing with objects, pooing in rage—or pretending to be appliances. What if the refrigerator tried to save the oven? "Don't be a hero, Fridge," became a classic line. That night, we got some Four Loko and drank it for research purposes. It tasted like cough syrup and, at 5 a.m., I was still wide awake, my blood like thunder. I remember being by the pool and (esteemed Esquire writer and all around awesome guy) Chris Jones laughing so hard he nearly barfed. It was one of the best times of my life. I wish we could all travel back to that weekend and live it again.

—Erin Sullivan

DATELINE: Austin, Texas

Under a canopy of trees by a neighborhood once known as Shadow Lawn, a family of artists lived in a bright blue bungalow. The family was called Fitzgerald.

Inside the bungalow, a trove of drawings, etchings, acrylics and photographs hung from the walls, but all of the artists were gone. Only their mother, who earned her keep as a midwife, was left to look at the artwork. The mother's name was Michele.

"I have three sons," she said, "who were all born at home."

The three sons of Michele Fitzgerald traced their talent to a great-uncle, Thomas Hart Benton, the painter best known for his depictions of the American Midwest. One of their maternal uncles designed murals for movie theaters; another turned a blighted neighborhood into a garden district. Their father, Kerry Fitzgerald, painted concert posters for the old Armadillo World Headquarters, birthplace of a celebrated music scene. Art was the family profession.

Not long after his fourth birthday, the youngest of the sons, who went by his middle name Jake, made a drawing of a musical robot. His mother kept the drawing in a special place on the bathroom wall for many years, long after her divorce. The allusion to his father's artistic path was hard to miss.

"Their dad was a muralist, so what were we going to do?" she said. "Now I feel like I might have set him up."

* * *

In this same city lived a detective, tall and jowly, nearing 50 years old with a slight paunch. The detective's name was Kevin Bartles.

Before joining the police force, Bartles had worked for radio stations in Nacogdoches, Tyler and other places. He enjoyed the lifestyle. He enjoyed the work. He played Top 40 hits, recordings made by established performers, promoted by entertainment conglomerates and acclaimed by mass purchase.

In the late 1980s, Bartles moved home to work as an emergency dispatcher. One day, in a moment of frustration, he asked permission to personally respond to an attack on an elderly woman. The supervisor said he would have to join the police academy if he wanted to do that sort of thing, so he did.

"I've tended," he said, "to be overly sympathetic with the victims."

After pursuing copper wire thieves on a property crimes detail, the detective turned his attention to vandalism. He spoke with neighborhood groups. He spoke with landlords. By his account, one shopkeeper told him: "I gave up on the police a long time ago. We don't even report it anymore. In the morning, we unlock the door, turn off the burglar alarm and get out the cans of paint to cover up the graffiti from the night before."

The detective developed a sense of moral outrage. He was not alone. Across the country, law enforcement agencies cast graffiti as the root of many woes. The Department of Justice estimates the cost at $12 billion a year, stifling retail sales, depressing home prices and inspiring gang membership.

Courts have started ordering prison time in place of fines and community service. Last year, a judge in Corpus Christi sentenced an 18-year-old to six years on graffiti charges.

For his part, Bartles worked 12-hour shifts. He volunteered for surveillance duty. He took snapshots. He studied subcultures. He documented styles. He organized the physical evidence into a wall chart.

But still there was the matter of motive, most vexing of all.

"I cringe," Bartles wrote in a slide show presented to judges and prosecutors, "when I hear someone refer to graffiti as 'graffiti art.'"

* * *

As a boy, Jake Fitzgerald called himself Knuckles. He ran around bare-bellied. He told his big brothers, "You're not the boss of me."

In middle school, he lifted weights, painted and found few friends. To jocks, he was the artsy weirdo; to art students, the dumb jock.

As his brothers pursued artistic careers in Oregon and New York, Jake attended four high schools in two years. He dropped out of 10th grade, earned a GED and lived with his mother. He covered the garage with images of spacemen.

"You could be an artist and promote yourself and make a living," Michele remembers telling him. "Don't just do a job to support your art hobby. It's a hard way to make a living, but it's a cop-out to say you can't."

Soon Jake's artwork grew more intricate. Characters recurred in new forms. A figure once depicted flying free appeared in chains.

At night, Jake smoked marijuana, roamed the streets and worried his mother, Michele recalls. He adopted his first street name, Saz. He started trying to think of a better name, one suggesting fame and glory.

Six times, he was arrested as a juvenile, according to court records. Adult charges followed, for joyriding and hard drugs. Offered deferred adjudication, he blew his chance. From Jan. 12 through Feb. 11, 2008, he was held in cells 23 and 31 of the Travis County Jail.

* * *

From chasing scrap metal thieves, Detective Bartles knew to focus on repeat offenders. Long prison sentences could send a message. In presentations to neighborhood watch groups, he argued against the kind of graffiti havens used in places like Venice Beach, Calif., and Queens, N.Y.

Bartles wrote: "Remember what the attractions are for the taggers: to become a well-known tagger in the area, to get away with doing something illegal and to do as much damage as possible."

Despite its utility in terms of criminal profiling, his observation misread a key element of the graffiti movement.

Building on the work of Dadaists, Surrealists and No!artists, who challenged traditional notions of artistic validity, early graffiti taggers added a powerful ultimatum. If Marcel Duchamp's famous urinal was not artwork, what was it? A conversation piece? Garbage? Plumbing?

But if spray paint on a wall was not art, it was clearly vandalism.

As galleries began to anoint such graffiti-inspired stylists as Jean-Michel Basquiat and Keith Haring, the artistic premise eroded. Adidas hired taggers to decorate a spring line. Sony used graffiti to promote the PlayStation.

And when the aesthetic gained mainstream acceptance, non-commercial graffiti became the province of common vandals. Civic leaders started regulating the sale of spray paint, among other measures.

To a younger generation, these developments point to a new golden age. Taggers such as Banksy, BNE and Neck Face cultivate certain associations with a sense of showmanship. They mark on walls; they provoke the police; they guard their identities like comic book villains. And their works sell at auction for thousands of dollars. Last summer, the Banksy film Exit Through the Gift Shop grossed more than $2 million.

Now, ambitious taggers market their street credibility through an online directory. It's called: "Art Crimes."

★ ★ ★

In 2008, Jake Fitzgerald escalated his criminal escapades. Caught fighting beneath a highway overpass, he was charged with aggravated assault, according to court records. Caught rolling a refrigerator down a dark street, he was charged with burglary.

"For Jake, it just snowballed," his mother said. "The more stuff that happened, the more they targeted him, the more he gave up."

When Jake appeared in court, his mother pleaded with the judge: A break from the streets, a family trip, an expanded horizon might yet turn him away from crime. The judge granted her plea.

In New Zealand, Jake studied computer art with an old family friend. Four months later, he returned to Texas with new skills.

On a website promoting his graffiti, Jake aimed to provoke, citing his hero as "that dude that shot those cops in oakland."

In a section for public comments, his friends applauded.

"OMG its KUDOS you're like so famous!" one admirer wrote. "Can I be your groupie??"

★ ★ ★

Around the courthouse, Detective Bartles was becoming a subject of curiosity. His affidavits spanned 20 pages of narrative, complete with color photographs and amateur handwriting analysis. Using distinctive flourishes to connect multiple pieces of graffiti to individual taggers, he was starting to build felony cases.

But even as grand juries endorsed his charges of aggregated vandalism, one prolific tagger seemed to be taunting him, posting photos of his own graffiti online.

Absent for several months, fresh instances of this tag were turning up around the city. Evenings in front of the TV, Bartles trawled the Internet on his laptop. He found pictures taken as far away as Wellington, New Zealand. Here was his big fish.

"You let that kind of thing go, it really fuels the fire," Bartles said. "Other taggers see him out there and nobody doing anything about it, they want that fame. And you have to decide: Are we serious about this?"

Bartles spread the word among law enforcement agencies: The tag he was after leaned to the left, with a squared bottom on the letter U and extended arms and legs to pierce the back line of the letter K.

Others noticed the return of the tag, too. On the website ATX Graffiti, one blogger wrote: "If you've been paying attention to Austin graff in 2009 you'll see that KUDOS is everywhere."

* * *

In the summer of 2009, Detective Bartles took a call from the Travis County Jail. More than a year earlier, the jailer told him, a guard inspecting a lower tier of the Baker Unit had documented some damage that might be of use to his investigation. Written in pencil on the windows, etched on the mirror and drawn around the sink and doorframe of cells 23 and 31, the marks matched the description Bartles was circulating.

"KUDOS—it's so compulsive he can't stop it," Bartles said. "In a jail cell, he's tagging. If you can't stop in a jail cell, what's wrong with you? It's almost like a male dog, they see a pole and they've got to do it."

From his files, Bartles compiled 44 instances of the KUDOS tag. Damage ranged from $34.28 (a trash can) to $480 (a railroad control building). The total came to $6,771.02, more than enough for a felony charge.

And county records showed that only one person had occupied both cells 23 and 31 during the time period in question. Bartles filed for a warrant to arrest one Robert Jake Fitzgerald, W/M, 11/24/1988.

"From all these pictures," Bartles wrote, "it's clear that Robert Fitzgerald uses the 'KUDOS' tag name and doesn't care who knows."

On Friday, Aug. 7, 2009, Bartles led an apprehension team in two unmarked cars to a bright blue bungalow, under a canopy of trees by a place once known as Shadow Lawn.

* * *

The youngest son of Michele Fitzgerald leans on his elbows. A white jumpsuit exaggerates his bright blue eyes, his big ears and his pallor. A tattoo on his left arm displays the area code 512, a bit of street tribalism usually associated with bigger cities. A tattoo on his right arm says "Detrimental."

After his arrest, court records show, he was bailed out by his mother, arrested again for theft and sentenced to 21 months in state jail, including six for graffiti vandalism.

Asked to describe his background, he mentions his travels, his father and his brothers. His main influence, he says, was a graffiti artist of some local prominence a decade ago.

"Back alleys where people don't walk, he'd be there, the forbidden areas of the city, the forgotten areas," he says. "You could tell he'd done some walking, he'd explored the city. People on their way to work would pass this tunnel full of beautiful artwork and not even know it's there."

He describes a code of honor learned on the streets.

"I wouldn't tag a church or a school or anybody's house," he says, an assertion not contradicted by the affidavit against him. "It's more the dirty part of the city: Dumpsters, rusty metal, alleys. Places the city's forgotten, is what our canvas becomes."

He speaks of a worthy adversary, a detective called Bartles, who has since been reassigned to the Organized Crime Division.

"He's just kind of known," Fitzgerald said. "You get into graffiti, and there's this side and there's that side."

Behind the walls of the Travis County State Jail, his services are in demand. He draws tattoos, he refines graffiti tags. His

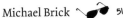

compensation comes in commissary credit and informal favors, but he harbors larger ambitions.

"There are places that'll pay for that, to have me do my logo on their wall," he says. "There are guys that make a living on it, going from art show to art show. But first you've got to come up through the streets, and be known that way. You get more respect that way; you're seen as more dedicated. And that's part of the fun of it. If all graffiti was legal, it wouldn't have that appeal.

"It would just be like any other artwork."

— *The Dallas Morning News*, April 9, 2011

Ex-N.F.L. Star Dreams of Taking Sports to Space

Was there ever a notion dumber than Float Ball? It was to be a game played in zero gravity. (Microgravity, to be precise, but let's not get all nitpicky.) Players, the pitch goes, would float and bounce against the walls and each other and dunk—all in ways impossible with earthbound sports, with a bonus "where you have to pick up a person holding a certain ball and throw them through a hoop as a sort of extra point."

Insane. For a number of reasons, not the least of which the general lack of availability of extended periods of microgravity for anyone outside of NASA, or who can throw away tens of millions of dollars on a visit to the International Space Station.

But there was Ken Harvey, a former linebacker with the Washington Redskins, promoting this game on a tour of a NASA facility in Maryland, touting a concept he called ("somewhat risibly," Mike notes) "Space Sportilization."

Who else but Mike would be writing about it? That is the beauty of a Brick story: Like so many of them, this one celebrates goofy dreamers with the loving hug of a Fountains of Wayne song and a barely perceptible wink. He profiles Harvey and explores the question of second acts for sports figures and throws in some information on space tourism. Sometimes, Harvey says, "you've got to believe the unbelievable."

And, in the few minutes it takes to read the piece, we're floating.

—John Schwartz

DATELINE: Greenbelt, Maryland

The game would be called Float Ball. It would combine elements of basketball, football and the Lionel Richie video for "Dancing on the Ceiling" into a sort of free-for-all, compelling weightless players to bounce off walls, obstacles and one another while herding weightless balls of various colors to either end of the playing space, which would be placed inside the cabin of a zero-gravity plane or, possibly, on the moon. Eventually, one day, if all went well, some sort of custom arena would be constructed. On Mars.

"There's a bonus," said the game's promoter, Ken Harvey, speaking to an attentive audience of National Aeronautics and Space Administration engineers, technicians and scientists at the Goddard Space Flight Center here recently, "where you have to pick up a person holding a certain ball and throw them through a hoop as a sort of extra point."

The football analogy seemed to come easily to mind. Ken Harvey was that Ken Harvey, No. 57 in your Washington Redskins program for much of the late 1990s. Playing linebacker during the largely highlight-free interregnum of Coach Joe Gibbs, Harvey made four appearances in the Pro Bowl.

Now 43, he has not played a down since he dropped out of training camp in 1999. This year, he took a day job in the front office, where he has been charged with serving, according to Redskins management, "as a resource and adviser in the development of responsibility initiatives."

With two sons nearing college age, Harvey has taken the steady, earthbound gig as an anchor while training his restless imagination on a high-concept project he has called, somewhat risibly, SpaceSportilization.

"I did things the hard way getting to the pros, and I'm doing things the hard way now," he said during an interview in a back room of the space center, where a disused model satellite served as decoration. "But sometimes you've got to believe the unbelievable."

For Harvey, the hard way had included dropping out of high school, working in a fast-food restaurant and rising through the junior college circuit before starting his career with the Phoenix Cardinals. After his run with the Redskins, there was talk of additional millions, then there were injuries and then there was talk of hundreds of thousands. He walked away from a shrinking pile of money into the booby-trapped netherworld of N.F.L. retirement.

While casting about as a motivational speaker, Harvey struck up a friendship with Allen Herbert, a fellow congregant at Grace Covenant Church in Chantilly, Va. Herbert, a consultant who studied aerospace engineering in college, encouraged him to consider the outer reaches of the tourism business.

In recent years, the space industry has turned increasingly to private sources of finance and inspiration. The Office of Commercial Space Transportation, a unit of the Federal Aviation Administration, has started licensing businesses for suborbital flights. One company, Virgin Galactic, has collected more than $25 million in deposits from about 250 prospective passengers.

Seeking his own role with some degree of skepticism, Harvey met with Eric Anderson, the president of Space Adventures, a private company in Vienna, Va., that has delivered six paying customers to the International Space Station.

"I've always been protective," Harvey said, "because everyone's always trying to use players."

Anderson, whose company also operates suborbital flights providing five minutes of weightlessness for $5,000, said in an interview that a Float Ball league would require a couple of decades of significant reductions in the cost of space travel. In the meantime, he said, thinking big can hardly hurt, least of all when the big thinker is a famous football player.

"Ken is a friend, and someone who has the ability to make things happen," Anderson said. "It just helps get people excited about space."

In the end, Harvey's inner Star Trek fan guided him away from the steakhouses and car dealerships of traditional N.F.L. retirement. Taking Herbert as a business partner, he set to work developing a futuristic movie, promoting envisioned athletic offshoots of extraterrestrial tourism and designing Float Ball. He has been invited to address the Global Space Technology Forum in Abu Dhabi next month.

Upon arrival here at the space flight center, on an invitation from the National Society of Black Engineers, Harvey excited a stir of autograph seekers in the security checkpoint.

Inside the campus, a collection of low-slung brick buildings dating to the 1950s, he was escorted on a tour of communications centers stranded in time, working rooms behind glass replete with mainframe computers, heavy phones and framed portraits of astronauts. The only thing missing seemed to be sweaty guys in thin neckties leaning over smoldering ashtrays. His guides spoke of long-ago flush times for space exploration in the cold war.

"You had somebody to compete against," Harvey said, "like Redskins against Cowboys."

When the time came for his presentation, Harvey descended the steps of a flag-decked auditorium. Stocky and bald-shaven, dressed in a patterned tie, gray suit, brown loafers and interlocking silver bracelets, he stood before a projection screen that displayed grainy images of the SpaceLab scientists performing gymnastic routines.

His audience, about 40 NASA specialists, fell silent. Harvey ran through a series of slides covering the troubled economy, the promise of space tourism, citations of sports in the work of science fiction novelists and precedent-setting events like Alan Shepard's lunar golf shot. He cracked jokes, digressed liberally and quickly won over the group.

"You may say, what the heck is all this?" Harvey told his audience. "You're talking about sports and entertainment complexes on the moon."

Advanced concepts like the Float Ball league, he argued, would develop in time from astronaut fitness programs, virtual reality games, zero-gravity flights and educational efforts designed to instill post-space age children with new interstellar dreams.

"Sometimes," he said, "it doesn't happen in your generation, but you plan to see it in the next generation."

Then the NASA employees quizzed Harvey on his strategy for making money from space sports, a goal that has largely eluded him so far. From the fifth row, Rosalyn Nelson, a thermal blanket technician, asked how the general public could afford games like Float Ball.

"Great, great, great question," Harvey said. "Next, please."

—*The New York Times*, October 31, 2008

Awaiting millions, brother fights for sister, their home

There is something joyously subversive that Michael Brick has managed to write the way he does in American newspapers—major American newspapers—for so long. He abides none of the usual standards of economy or structure or even punctuation. I can imagine one of his editors receiving his copy and thinking, "Didn't I assign this guy a brief?" I can imagine another hollering across the newsroom, "Hey Brick, have you ever heard of THE FUCKING COMMA!" (If such a bullheaded character were named Mr. Brick in a movie, it would be a little too on the nose. Thankfully real life doesn't much care about its audience.) But Brick the writer, like Brick the man, isn't lawless. He follows many rules; they just happen to be his own. This story, about a family's long fight against an oil company, written in the midst of his own titanic struggle, demonstrates so perfectly the Brick Code: Ordinary people are the most deserving of extraordinary language. His hundreds of subjects over the years have so been given a gift. By fate of newsroom assignment, they won the company of an empathetic man who feels that the people to whom we afford the least notice deserve the most of his. I don't expect Minerva Ramirez has any notion that a stranger came into her house and took careful measure of her obsession with Tinkerbell and then wrote a story that made his readers want to run through a wall on her behalf. That doesn't make her, or any of us, any less fortunate for however long we enjoyed Mr. Brick's attentions.

—Chris Jones

DATELINE: Laredo, Texas

Minerva Ramirez wears her fine hair in a floral bow, pretty like Tinkerbell. At her brother's house in South Texas, she watches slapstick comedy videos, sings along to Michael Jackson and serves her dolls tea on Tinkerbell placemats. At night, she sleeps under Tinkerbell sheets.

"She can't tell time," says her brother, Leon Ramirez Jr., "but she has Tinkerbell on her wristwatch."

At 62, Minerva has long outlived the predictions of her doctors, despite the complications of aging with Down syndrome. She hugs strangers and calls any woman with gray hair "Abuela." In the electronics aisle at Kmart, Leon videotapes her dancing to the music of display stereos.

Leon pledged to take care of his sister, and he has. But Minerva seems to know little of her brother's worries. He is fighting to save their home, as mortgage debts have eroded the family's finances.

By Leon's account, supported by the ruling of an exasperated judge, petroleum companies owe them millions of dollars for wells drilled on property inherited from their grandmother. The main defendant, ConocoPhillips of Houston, has refused to pay, filing multiple appeals including one to the state Supreme Court. A co-defendant, EOG, also of Houston, has settled its role. Both firms declined comment.

Judge Joe Lopez of 49th state district court has chastised lawyers for ConocoPhillips and other parties for making redundant attacks "under the disguise of allegedly newly discovered evidence."

Oil and gas companies have developed a reputation over the years for tenacious legal defenses. As Texas braces for a long bust in its most important industry, legal observers say energy companies will play even tougher in the courtroom to protect their financial interests. For some landowners whose royalty payment agreements have turned sour, the legal fight likely will drag on with no end in sight.

"In any case where significant money is involved,... companies often feel an obligation to litigate so that a settlement doesn't become precedent and routine," said William Keffer, an oil and gas expert who lectures at Texas Tech University School of Law.

As the industry has consolidated into giant corporations with vast resources, energy companies have deployed increasingly sophisticated strategies in prominent environmental lawsuits, including the Exxon Valdez spill in 1989 and the BP Deepwater Horizon blowout in the Gulf of Mexico five years ago.

While big spills make big headlines, petroleum companies deal more frequently with a different area of law: contracts. Surveying 800 corporate lawyers for a report in May, the law firm Norton Rose Fulbright found that 45 percent of energy companies listed contracts as a top legal concern, compared to 34 percent for other industries.

"The structure of this industry with landowners, royalty owners, oil companies, customers and on through the midstream and downstream relies on a series of contracts among parties whose interests are not always aligned," said Bruce Bullock, director of the Maguire Energy Institute at Southern Methodist University. "The sheer number of interests results in more litigation."

* * *

The Ramirez family of Zapata County built a life in the brushlands of the early 20th century, running cattle on a tract of land near the border. They called it Las Piedras Ranch. There they raised three children, who gave them grandchildren. Minerva came along in 1953.

"She was my dad's favorite," said her brother, Leon Jr. "That's fine with us, because we love her, too."

Minerva and Leon grew up in Laredo, away from life on the ranch. Their grandfather died in 1966; their grandmother followed in 1988. A few years later, oil companies leased the right to drill on Las Piedras Ranch. Gas wells flourished. Millions of dollars flowed. The Ramirezes all received royalties based on mineral rights.

Minerva's father, Leon Sr., invested his share poorly, according to the family's lawyer, Alberto Alarcon. He took on hefty mortgage loans to buy old apartment buildings, hotels and truck stops.

By the time the recession arrived, the wells had run dry, Alarcon said. Debts accrued. Banks foreclosed on some properties;

the IRS placed liens on others. "They're about to lose everything," Alarcon said.

Then some old documents came to light.

* * *

To drill for oil and gas, energy companies must first determine who owns the minerals buried underground.

Over generations, by inheritance or sale, mineral rights frequently become separated from ownership of the land. In the oil boom that ended last year, industry researchers known as landmen packed courthouses across the state, seeking to determine the proper owners to sign mineral contracts.

As petroleum companies and landowners come to terms with a price crash that has made drilling less profitable, settling the legacy of those hastily drawn contracts has fallen to the courts.

"Royalty owners will be motivated to scrutinize their royalty statements more closely, to make sure they are getting what they're owed," Keffer said, "and there will be no shortage of plaintiff's lawyers ready to confirm that that's the case."

In Texas, where the industry contributes billions of dollars to the tax base and employs hundreds of thousands of people, legal experts say, petroleum company lawyers can find themselves emboldened by sympathetic officials.

"Texas appellate court decisions have been largely favorable to oil and gas producers, not just the big ones but any of them, for 100 years," said Bruce Kramer, a lawyer who advises corporate energy companies for McGinnis Lochridge of Houston.

But every case is judged on its own merits, Kramer said, and companies have a right to decide how to represent their interests in court.

"As any ongoing enterprise would do, they're going to make a business decision on whether it's important to fight or if it's okay to settle."

* * *

Grandmother Leonor Ramirez, the matriarch known as Mama No-ne, had left behind a small amount of stock. It finally drew the attention of the family around 2010, Alarcon said, when the executor of her will faced her own final days.

Hired to help settle ownership of the stock, Alarcon consulted the grandmother's will. To her daughter had gone clothing, jewelry and some property in Laredo. To one son, Leon Sr., the father of Minerva and Leon Jr., had gone a car and the land at Las Piedras Ranch. Upon his death, she wrote, "the title shall vest in his children then living in equal shares."

Her other son, Rodolfo Ramirez, received a one-third portion of any remaining property. According to Alarcon, Rodolfo made his own separate arrangements with ConocoPhillips and EOG, also of Houston.

In a 1997 letter, a senior land adviser for Conoco wrote to Rodolfo suggesting a recalculation. Instead of just his own established mineral rights, Rodolfo's portion would expand to include mineral rights connected to the land belonging to Grandmother Leonor. The adviser provided a stipulation for family members to sign.

"Rapidly on the very next day," Alarcon wrote in a civil complaint, "Rodolfo reported to his conspiracy principal, Conoco, that the transgression had been accomplished, and demanded his share of the loot."

The oil companies never had a valid lease on the grandmother's land, Alarcon wrote. Enlisting Rodolfo to trick his niece and nephew, he argued, the companies held onto millions of dollars that should have gone to Minerva and Leon Jr. The judge agreed with Alarcon that this tactic amounted to a conspiracy.

Rodolfo Ramirez could not be reached for comment, and his lawyer didn't return phone calls.

In court filings, ConocoPhillips argued that changes in the state probate code invalidate Leon and Minerva Riveras' claim to ownership of the grandmother's mineral rights. Further, the company noted, business had proceeded for more than 20 years in good faith before their wing of the family sued to obtain a new and improper interpretation of the will.

"Two generations in the Ramirez family now dispute the meaning of Leonor's will," wrote lawyers for ConocoPhillips. "They have no claim."

* * *

Minerva's Tinkerbell sheets are tucked into a hospital bed now. Since she stopped eating a few years ago, a feeding tube delivers nutrients into her abdomen. An oxygen device supplements her breathing. Twice a week, she receives visits from a nurse and a therapist. She uses a walker to hand out candy at Halloween.

"My dad knew that Minerva would never be put in a home or an institution," said Leon Jr. "There's a real person, a real human being in Minerva ..."

His voice trailed off. The promises he made to his father are getting harder to keep. Since Nov. 19, 2010, he has been fighting the oil companies and his uncle in court. After multiple rounds of appeals and judgments—all in his favor—little has been resolved.

"This case was litigated for over four years," Lopez wrote. Each time ConocoPhillips lost, the judge noted, the company tried to start over by challenging jurisdiction, turning the lawsuit into a probate proceeding and deploying other baseless tactics.

On May 11, 2015, Lopez signed an order directing ConocoPhillips to pay Minerva $3.7 million, plus attorney's fees of $1.1 million. The order was titled, "Final Judgment." ConocoPhillips has appealed.

"Maybe I would've given up years ago, but I know Minerva needs somebody to stand and fight for her," Leon Jr. said. "And we want Conoco to do the right thing."

Now he is running out of time. The IRS has posted the family home for foreclosure sale on Oct. 29.

—*The Houston Chronicle*, October 25, 2015

PART TWO: PLACES

Where Summer Glides Down Like a 9 A.M. Beer

Mike Brick is an original. That's an easy thing to say, and it's been said about so many artists that it comes off as almost trite. No one is reinventing the language; there are still only 26 letters in the alphabet. Most of us are doing our best to imitate the tried and true. But there are a few who manage to leave their imprint on those well-worn styles, whose voices cannot be stifled or assimilated into the template. That's Mike Brick.

For example, when I first met Brick in 2009, he was this tall, quiet Texan, sizing up strangers through trademark aviators from the back of a room full of egos. As the sun set, the music started to trickle out, everyone taking hacks at Dylan and Springsteen until Brick emerged with a ragged spiral-bound, grabbed a guitar, and announced his presence with an original song—short, three simple chords in a standard progression, but lyrics that were raw and sincere:

Waitress hand all that good whiskey down
I guess I always stayed around
And who in this land is alone?
The answers are never known

No one wanted to follow him.

That introductory scene made more sense as I read more of Brick's stories. He goes to a place like Ruby's Old Thyme Bar and Grill in Coney Island and hangs back, no first person, no heavy-handed internal exposition, *just taking in details, setting the scene. Allowing characters like Willy the bartender to sketch herself through the act of emptying her pockets and her words: "But people give me stuff all day."*

Brick, the narrator, is invisible—until he sees his opportunity to briefly interject: Some days a beer brings a taste of being 15 years old; some days it just tastes like another beer.

Who wants to follow that?

—Tony Rehagen

Way behind the black-and-white roller coaster pictures and smiling beer girl posters, the snapshots of the regulars and the late lamented Ruby, a sign behind the bar said, "Welcome Back to Coney Island Summer 2004." The scrawny dude everybody calls Master was walking around in a too-big tank top looking for a good place to hang a new sign. Same message, different summer.

There was Willy behind the bar, same job for 24 years. Her daddy was William, who wanted a son; she's Willy the lady bartender. She has 90 bottles of liquor, 75 bottles of wine and no visible end of beer. Anything that won't get you drunk is somebody else's job. Willy empties her pockets when she works. It bothers her, walking around with stuff in her pockets.

"But people give me stuff all day," she said.

It was nothing a smoke break wouldn't fix: Summer was coming on fast at Ruby's down by the Boardwalk. In a city of close quarters, a bar is a mystery nobody wants to solve, a hiding place and a box social, where everybody knows that nobody knows your name. There are scads of them, but Ruby's is the summer place, open 9 a.m. to whenever, April to Halloween, a Woody in a minivan world.

Like any good dive, Ruby's has its regulars and its history, but those are other stories. This is the story of another long slide into summertime at Ruby's Old Thyme Bar and Grill, Coney Island, Brooklyn, New York City, U.S.A.

There are dark bars and bright bars, and Ruby's is both. The vibe changes like the watercolor smear that is summertime. The room is an airy gap, three walls and a pair of garage doors facing the beach. The bar top is long and dark, wide enough to keep three feet between you and Willy.

Behind it are dolls, a toy panda, a bust of Harpo Marx, the kind of stuff they give away at arcades around the corner to make kids think their parents are winners. This is where the regulars sit, across from Willy on the sunny end by the Boardwalk. They hunch or lean, shoulder blades pointing to the kitchen, where college kids sell the Coney Island lunch wagon, clams and corn dogs and the rest.

Two days into summertime, the crew was getting ready for the biggest blowout of the year. The Mermaid Parade brings out the amateur weird by the thousands for a strut by the shore. "It's going to be nuts on Saturday, huh?" a customer asked Mike Sorrell, a son-in-law of Ruby's and a manager of the bar.

"And it's going to be 90 degrees," Mr. Sorrell said.

A young woman was standing at the middle of the bar going through her purse, making a show of it. After a few minutes of nobody buying her a beer, she found her money. Down where the regulars sit, a breeze blew some bills down the bar. Willy caught them.

"Here, it's back here now," she said, stacking the cash by the register. That was where it was going anyway.

Saturday, June 25, came bright, and the tables looked like a group photo of Brooklyn, black kids slurping sodas across from a blond woman with a Corona next to Asian teenagers eating hot dogs. It was 90 degrees. Master, aka Genaro Rivera, 56, was in full Puerto Rican get-up, a flag-colored tank-top down to his knees and a floppy hat to match. "Sometimes we get a little trouble," Master said, grinning like a maniac, "but I control it."

Over by the jukebox, Howie Willis, 45, was dancing to Sinatra with a woman named Patty. His T-shirt said Sloppy Joe's Fishing Team.

"Tomorrow it won't be nearly as crowded, but the guys I know 20 years will be here," said Mr. Willis, who comes to Ruby's a few times a summer. He was saying he was proud to have his picture on the wall. Patty was saying he ought to shut up.

"I just met her," Mr. Willis said, "and now I'm cut off."

Out on the Boardwalk, a guy painted blue and carrying a trident was putting away an onion dog, surrounded by girls in green sequined bras pressed up against girls with rainbow wigs and guys with Mardi Gras beads. They were supposed to be mermaids. They were putting away Buds.

A breeze was coming off the ocean. Patty made her way toward the Boardwalk. Within two feet of the door, she fainted in the heat. Some jerk in a Mets cap started counting her out, but better men helped her to a bench by a fan. She was fine.

The sun was on its slow way down, but people were still coming past the echoing clang of the batting cage and the wind and the waves.

Summertime: It was too late to stop now. The long hot slide had begun, but summer at Ruby's is no picture postcard. Two days after the parade, the doors framed a sky the color of mock turtle soup.

A pattering rain fell on the beach. Some days a beer brings a taste of being 15 years old; some days it just tastes like another beer. The regulars had been gone since noon. Theresa Hoha, wearing her given name on her necklace, was taking a day off from the housekeeping service she runs on Long Island.

"I don't want to take my life for granted," Ms. Hoha said. "I'm glad for what I've got. I'm glad when the sun comes out, and I'm glad to see the moon and stars."

From behind the kitchen counter, Robin Mates, 25, called for somebody to put number 8001 on the jukebox for Willy. Kenny Rogers started singing about advice that had cost him a last swallow of whiskey: "Every hand's a winner, and every hand's a loser, and the best that you can hope for is to die in your sleep."

Then the song was done and the Long Islanders went the way of the regular crowd. Willy said she was closing; there were going to be other summer days.

—*The New York Times*, July 3, 2005

Finding Shade
in a Legend's Shadow

First off: Dude has a great byline. That matters. You might skip a story by James L. Smith III. But you've got to at least try out a Michael Brick. And once you try one Michael Brick, you're hooked.

For years, somehow, he got these ballads of normal life among normal human beings published in The New York Times, which you can scan for an hour some days without finding the kind of person you might ever run into on the street. The stories are beautifully written, yes, but more than that they're beautifully reported. Here is his one and only sentence describing a particular barfly at Ruby's on Coney Island:

To Master, aka Genaro Rivera; in June he hung Mermaid Day banners, now he sits wanting to quit smoking Viceroys while one lung still works.

Twenty-four words and now there is a picture in your head of Genaro Rivera, as vivid as a ViewMaster. The writing comes from the reporting, and the reporting comes from paying attention. There's no one way great writers get the job done, but most of them end up in the same place: Everybody's interesting, and every person matters. That's how the world really is. And that's how it feels in Michael Brick's hands.

Years ago, in a group of guys with guitars trading songs, Brick did Michael Jackson's "Man In the Mirror." It's a song I'd always mocked in my mind—Make that change! Cha-mon!— but Brick played it quiet and intense, and the heart of it flowed out of him. He took a corny-ass song, made famous by an earthly alien, and found the humanity inside both. That's why you read Michael Brick once, and all you want to do is keep reading.

—Tommy Tomlinson

DATELINE: Long Island, New York

Machpela Avenue is patched and pebbled, and you have to walk past Mitchell Parish 1900-1993 Lyricist, past gates to the Abion Sick and Benevolent Society and past scattered stones where the grass stretches open to get to where Ruby has gone.

"Loved and Admired, a Friend to All," his gravestone at Beth David Cemetery on Long Island says, and the Parachute Drop and the Wonder Wheel and the Cyclone are suspended in low relief before the legend: "Coney Island the Elixer of Life."

The stone says Rubin Jacobs is gone five summers to Machpela Avenue, but some tell it that he is not there at all. His likeness hangs over Ruby's Old Thyme Bar and Grill on the Coney Island Boardwalk, a 40-minute ride away, where now comes the middle of Summer No. 6 without him—a long, slow burn, a weary interval for legends and talk of end times.

Ruby's on a midsummer afternoon is a good thing for Philly and Sammy and Norma and Master: old-timers getting older on either side of the counter, down by the shore where Ruby waved his metal detector on the impossible sands and found treasures and some days found nothing. In a photograph, Ruby feeds birds some 1980's summer day, and Sammy Rodriguez indicates this picture when he speaks of the man.

"He's watching you," Mr. Rodriguez says, and his authority is known because he worked here before Ruby's was Ruby's. He was here in the 1950's when the choices were Rheingold and Schaefer and Pabst Blue Ribbon and none besides. Here when Ruby's was a Hebrew National restaurant, and here during the big fire in the 1970's when the mahogany counter burned and all the mirrors burned and the walls and the ceiling and the seven beer taps.

Mr. Rodriguez was here when Ruby Jacobs, owner of a camera shop in the city, took over the bathhouses by the shore, here when nobody came to the bathhouses anymore and the bathhouses closed, here in the 1980's when Ruby took over the bar. Ruby's has no taps, only bottles, and where the old bar had mirrors, now there are photographs, hundreds of them.

The top ones show fading scenes of Dreamland Tower and Shooting the Chute; the bottom ones are brilliant glossies of late vintage such that you might be on that wall, too. Are you the redhead with high cheekbones at the Mermaid Parade? Did you paint your lips blue or wear seashells on your breasts? Were you in stilettos or a feathered bikini? Did you pout to the camera some hot forgotten day?

A bar with photographs is a bar with memories, and everybody tells the Ruby stories: Ruby put a wounded pigeon into a cage on the counter to heal, and inspectors came and Ruby paid a fine for his good deed. Ruby found a man breaking into Ruby's and asked the man why'd he do it, and the man said he needed money and Ruby gave him a job. Maybe the stories are true but you don't know.

In late July, Ruby's is a good thing, too, for tourists and homeboys and families and deathless Dodger fans, but a good thing is just like a bad thing when it comes to what you say about it. A blackout, a famine, Cal Ripken on a streak, the secret of Deep Throat, Marah singing "Freedom Park," the expanding universe: You say how long will it last and will this be the year it ends, and this kind of talk makes midsummer go by at Ruby's.

"I hope they don't come in and knock everything down and make Disneyland," says Catherine DeSimone. "Knock everything else down, but don't knock down Ruby's."

And as summer is short but the middle days long, so Ruby's remains but the faces change. Here's to Norma, who sat in the corner with Betty, who wore white gloves and spoke of baseball; now Norma sits alone. To Master, aka Genaro Rivera; in June he hung Mermaid Day banners, now he sits wanting to quit smoking Viceroys while one lung still works. To Philly Sanalitro, who has blood behind his eyeball; he just turned 78 and his heart is no good.

"I'm all messed up, I'm like a can opener," Mr. Sanalitro says. He quit smoking and drinking but here he is anyway, saying: "You know what, I'm happy, I want to live long. I'm not married, I got no worries."

And here's to Willy the pretty lady bartender; she looks better late in July after the shots for the cancer in her stomach. To Sammy Rodriguez, who says he will go home to Puerto Rico before Ruby's closes for the season on Halloween.

"I'm not saying I'm quitting," Mr. Rodriguez says on the last Tuesday in July, "but my body is saying no mas."

He is kidding maybe, and he gets a laugh from Frank Chmielowski, the 56-year old teacher and coach who comes back to Brooklyn from Santa Rosa, Tex., in midsummer to drink with friends from long ago. Frankie knows the talk around Ruby's; he was here the week before, speculating on the end.

"It's only going to be two more years before they tear it all down," he says, and then a girl on the Boardwalk walks by wearing a thong and you can see her tattoo.

Frankie drinks his beer and the jukebox is quiet. Willy the lady bartender opens the metal register and pushes some bills down and says she always has to keep track of everything. Frankie points to a picture of Ruby on the wall. There he is, he says. He looks out at the Boardwalk and the bikinis and the green trash cans like slalom cones, and he says Brooklyn girls are a little rough around the edges.

"Texas is known for its beautiful women," he mentions, and his drinking companion says that's a fact, Jack. Then the jukebox gets paid and the idle talk stops and all you can hear is Maurice Williams and the Zodiacs saying your daddy don't mind and your mommy don't mind if we have another dance just one more time.

— *The New York Times*, August 7, 2005

Last Call on the Boardwalk, Perhaps Forever

Brick's reporter friends at the Times raised their brows when word got out that he was spending the summer of 2005 reporting— we'd say it with quotations, like this: "reporting"—and writing a series about hanging out at the beach bar Ruby's. This was maybe a little too good a fit? Sending Mike Brick to write about a dive bar in Brooklyn was like assigning a story about the North Pole to Santa Claus. But Brick had a knack for approaching the familiar as if he had stumbled on a lost tribe or a new planet. And then reporting back to the good people of Earth. Dateline: Uranus. Dateline: Kings County Supreme Court. Dateline: Coney Island. Wherever. We were privileged, as neighbors of Brick's in the newsroom and a couple of the smaller offices at the city bureaus, to front-row season tickets to his departures into the field—"Wish me luck, boys!"—and his returns, sometimes triumphant, sometimes empty-handed, never dull in his telling.

What news, then, from Ruby's?

Brick capped off his Coney Island triptych with this masterful weave of the low and the high, the dirty floor and the night sky, the rim-shot one-liners ("Master smokes Viceroys, but he doesn't turn down gifts") and the swell of the orchestra as the curtain drops, with a final sentence too good to rip out of context and drop here. The assignment that could have been too good a fit wasn't too good at all, but just right.

—Michael Wilson

DATELINE: Coney Island, New York

Philly Sanalitro said he got a phone call from beyond the great divide. This guy who had been trying to kill him was there on the line, and the guy called Philly "Big Jim."

"I pick it up: 'Hello, Big Jim,'" Philly said. He was standing next to the bar at Ruby's telling this story, and he told it mostly the same all summer long. It was the late summer heat wave and he was wearing a white bandanna and he had another one in his pocket, but he had left his wallet at home.

Philly's face sags off his nose and he spits when he talks. He leans in and he hits his chest and he worries his hands together, and his blue cap blocks the abominable sun. He said the man on the phone told him: "'Hey, my friend, I'm dead.'

"I said, 'How can you be dead? You're talking to me.'

"He said, 'I'm in heaven, I'm dead.'

"I told the guy: 'What's it look like?'

"'People singing, and music. Like a band singing.'"

"I didn't hear nothing."

Philly finishes talking and goes home before sundown, and when the sun goes down nighttime is something different at Ruby's Old Thyme Bar and Grill on the Coney Island Boardwalk. At Ruby's maybe nothing ever dies, but summer sneaks off in the middle of the night. You wake up and you can't get it back; it's gone.

Nighttime at Ruby's is this: The sand and the gulls and the wind and the waves masked, and clear lines between brightness and dark. Inside, fluorescent lamps shine on the beer girl posters and the old-time photographs and the purblind man selling toilet paper by the ladies' lavatory. Outside, small bulbs in the blackness describe the faraway roller coaster and the patrol car parked on the wooden slats.

It's late in the day, late in the season, and Ruby's is on borrowed time six summers now; Ruby Jacobs dead and buried. His daughter, Cindy, has a day job, and she left Sammy Rodriguez to run things this summer the way he has for years. All around new money is coming into Coney Island, and Cindy does not say what she will do. Her old

friend Catherine DeSimone walks around with a camera taking movies just in case.

Sometimes Willy the lady bartender ends her shift at sundown and Sammy stays and tends bar himself. He says the summers are getting longer. He kept the place open Aug. 10 for Victor Deyglio and Lexi Gray to celebrate their anniversary; they had married at Ruby's with the huckster next door shouting congratulations. The sword swallower and the bed-of-nails man came to the party, and Victor sat at the bar and his wife rode the roller coaster around and around.

"She can just sit in the car because they know her," Victor said.

When Lexi came back she was wearing a blue dress and glitter makeup and a watchband but no watch. The wine bottles on the table were empty, and Sammy was bringing in the chairs.

"We're sitting in this beautiful limbo of the past catching up with us and the future encroaching," Lexi said. Then somebody found a praying mantis on the Boardwalk and the party studied it and Sammy turned out the lights.

Summertime: The end was coming soon. Sammy would go home to Puerto Rico and Willy was talking about moving to Kansas. Frank Chmielowski, who watched the beach from the corner of the bar, would go back to Santa Rosa, Tex., and the regulars would find someplace else to drink.

The last Friday in August the bumper boats were closed and the wind was blowing off the beach. The sun was going down on the right. The skinny dude everybody calls Master, aka Genaro Rivera, was wearing floppy socks and a white sailor's cap.

"For the young people saying Wepa, it went fast," Master said, using an island word he employs to describe fireworks, Puerto Rico, beauty, Ruby's, the ocean, Coney Island, metal detectors, youth, a punch in the gut, a phone call late at night, duty, honor, truth, time, deception, silence and Friday nights. Then he started inviting people to his 27th birthday party, which took place three decades ago.

Vicki Weathersby with the bright pink lipstick and the feathered purse traded her Nathan's Famous cup for a beer. Somebody was blowing soap bubbles and the bubbles were coming into the bar. On the jukebox Ray Charles was singing "I got a woman way over town she's good to me." The crowd was trying to guess Master's age.

"Let's cut him open and count the rings," Vicki called. She squeezed his chest in her arms and a pack of Marlboros stuck up in his shirt pocket. Master smokes Viceroys, but he doesn't turn down gifts. He was standing on the line where the wooden slats are painted red and the Boardwalk ends and Ruby's starts. "We-pa!" Master said, and he raised his voice like a tent show healer:

"I seen the babies born, I seen the babies grow. When I came to this world nobody was expecting me," he said, and then he lifted his arms and he repeated, "He visto a los bebes nacidos, he visto que los bebes crecen. Cuando yo vine a este mundo que nadie me esperaba."

The sun was gone and a man walked by carrying a boa constrictor and a kid did a break dance and a girl in a low-cut shirt pulled the zipper up her sweater.

"Another summer bites the dust," Cindy Jacobs said. Master swallowed a double shot of whiskey and put his finger to his lips. Out in the blackness the rockets came without preamble in tracers of gold and green and carnival noise, squalling and fitful, bass and snare of a piece and voices ascending and no music and Vicki sitting there clapping without a sound.

—*The New York Times*, September 4, 2005

Where Doves, and the Threat of Danger, Fill the Air

Doves, American sportsmen, and Mexican drug cartels: What's not to love, and envy, about this Brick gem. Honestly. It's not just the laser beam of our correspondent's eye, or deft writer's hand; what gives the deepest pleasure here is that Brick has found himself—nay, willingly put himself—in a strange, dangerous pocket of the world (Sinaloa, Mexico... "cartel country") and created an eyewitness evocation, spotted a once-invisible fable here. From the "gaunt roosters" patrolling to the ringing truth of the story's last violent line, everything takes on a shimmer that occurs when worlds collide, when the unwitting enter a fraught paradise. It's the kind of piece that you might read a few times because it's so carefully constructed and playing with so many ideas (entitlement, joy, muffled fear...). For me, the upfront bit of dialogue—"It's not good to be macho."—somehow rings mysteriously throughout. These are not Hemingway heroes, then. And this is not some idyllic garden. Here, we realize, the larger metaphor: these American hunters are hunted, too. But the lingering question remains: Do they know as much?

—Michael Paterniti

DATELINE: Ahome, Mexico

The hunting party set out Sunday morning through unlit fog. Molded shotgun cases slid around the van underfoot. Numbered buckets held 12,000 unspent cartridges. The trapped air smelled of insect repellent.

The outfitter, Dave Warner, held the wheel. He is 61, a reformed drinker with a gold-gray bowl haircut, thick crow's feet and stubby Popeye arms. He steered through the predawn stillness past tumble-down shanties where gaunt roosters patrolled. Outside town, a red pickup truck carrying eight riders accelerated to race.

"The gringo by a nose," one of the hunters called.

A hurrah was given.

"No," Warner said, almost to himself. "It's not good to be macho."

Through his side window appeared the unfinished construction of a gated showpiece, a mansion rising among the shacks.

"This was either drug money or coyote money," he said. "I'm not sure which."

The hunters rode on, eager to inaugurate the four-month dove season. Here in the cartel country of Sinaloa State, not far from the Sea of Cortez, they had been promised some of the most bountiful bird grounds in the world. They had been told of abundant mourning and white-winged populations, mostly virgin each autumn, cast in flight against mesmerizing landscapes through the temperate winter passage.

Drawn for generations to the Valle del Fuerte range, serious bird hunters have started adapting their operations as the government has taken on violent drug gangs, including the powerful Sinaloa Cartel. After a gun battle last month, the Mexican authorities arrested Jesus Zambada, known as the King, a Sinaloa underboss accused of trafficking cocaine and methamphetamine. Then last weekend, as dove season began, nearly a dozen police officers were killed. The acting federal police commissioner announced his resignation, accused of allowing the cartel to infiltrate his force.

Gone now are the loosely organized hunting trailer parks of an earlier time, places where American casino impresarios and retired military hands would camp for months on end, assembling for nightly smorgasbords.

"You just smuggled a gun in," said Warner, a native of Washington State whose father started hunting here in the early 1950s. "We'd drink cheap Champagne, listen to Dean Martin tapes, and that was it."

In place of those campgrounds, outfitters have constructed hunting lodges resembling army compounds. Brick walls stand 14 feet high, gates 18 or more, topped with barbed wire. To avoid the trouble of modern airline security, firearms and ammunition have been stocked for rental. Allegiances have been struck with the hopelessly outgunned local police.

The three-day hunt with Warner costs $1,795. For hunters, the rewards include a malleable limit of 60 birds in possession a day, twice the amount enforced in Texas and triple that of California. Plentiful across North America, doves have flourished in the breadbasket of western Mexico, where vast fields of sesame, corn and watermelon grow alongside broad canals. When lacking a market, many of the crops rot unharvested, visible from the road. And besides, government policy requires outfitters to spread feed mixture, a practice that could result in jail sentences for baiting in many parts of the United States.

Told of all this, the hunting party arrived Saturday, amid the Dia de los Muertos celebrations. Ranchers from small towns in and around Mendocino County, Calif., flew from Sacramento through Los Angeles and Hermosillo to the nearest airport, in Los Mochis. They arrived outside Warner's compound, Campo David, where a sign on the gate proclaimed: "Alta a la violencia."

Stop the violence.

If the hunters took notice, they did not say. Under a row of mounted antlers, bear and moose heads, they dined on roast pork, pico de gallo, mashed potatoes and fresh tortillas.

"Let it be a good hunt," Warner said.

Across the table sat Page Baldwin Jr., away from his young children on a fifth annual trip, this time to introduce his friends to the range. There was Joe DaCruz, among the youngest at 48, a world traveler up for a good time. There were Duncan McCormack III and

IV, shooting together to strengthen frayed paternal bonds. And there were Bill Mailliard, 66, and Larry Mailliard, 55, cousins to Baldwin, both doing their best to ignore back injuries.

At 4:30 Sunday morning, the hunters assembled in the courtyard. They taped their thumbs against the blisters of reloading 20-gauge Italian-made shotguns and wore shoulder pads to absorb the mild but repetitive kick. Soon the local teenagers hired to retrieve downed birds arrived at the gate, exciting the dogs and Yaki, Warner's pet monkey. Roosters crowed in the distance.

The first hunting ground was an hour's drive across rugged terrain. Vast fields of sesame lay ruined by Hurricane Norbert, the year's only crop left to the birds. The men stepped out near an estuary good for roosting.

"Paloma, paloma," someone called. Dove, dove.

The parcel was flat and rocky and the sky cloudless, painting the birds against a backdrop of solid blue. But the morning fog held, discouraging flight. The doves came one by one, as if testing the sky. They flew without pattern, swerving and shifting elevation like some cartoon knuckleball.

The hunters swung their barrels to aim above the mesquite trees, leading the birds by 10 feet or more. Firing a four-foot-diameter pattern to ensure clean kills, their range was limited to about 50 yards.

"Let 'em get here," Baldwin called.

Waiting, tracing, aiming skyward, DaCruz felled a bird directly overhead. The creature sputtered like a half-bladed helicopter and landed on its breast in the red dirt. It lifted its head three times, turned its neck to the right and died beside a yellow shell casing.

After an hour, the hunters had bagged only 125 birds, not much more than 20 a man. One of their hired hands, Jesus Espinoza, 17, stumbled across a rattlesnake, which Warner slew with a carefully calibrated shotgun blast. The hunters returned to the van.

"That place, normally you shoot double," Baldwin told his companions. "That's the slowest I've ever seen it."

On the road, Warner stopped to greet a police patrol. As he drove away, the lead officer waved along the hunting party's hired hands, a group of Mexican teenagers driving a van with American plates.

"He's a good friend of mine," Warner said.

Back at the compound, the Mexican workers took the birds to a white tile room with broad metal sinks. They removed the head, feet and one wing of each bird, leaving the other intact to distinguish species.

In the afternoon the hunters drove to a valley where craggy hillsides pocked with caverns set a confounding backdrop.

"When they kidnapped a friend of mine out here, they got away so quick that they thought they had him hiding up in one of those caves," Warner said.

A hawk descended, stirring the prey. Reports resounded across the valley.

"Holy cow," said the younger McCormack. "It's just buzzing with them."

Somebody asked Warner to continue the kidnapping story.

"Three months, blindfolded the whole time," he concluded.

Later there would be a great celebration in the van, with the recounting of certain shots, the bestowing of nicknames and bottles of tequila and Jack Daniel's passed hand to hand. There would follow a feast of tender dove breast cooked on kabob with bacon, onion and bell pepper. The hunters would go home to California with coolers of sinewy meat, some for a school fund-raiser.

But first, they returned the next dawn to the valley, where the birds flew in great waves, beating their wings and showing their white bellies and soaring through the towering cacti as six shotgun barrels warmed to a great and guttural chorus.

"Yee-ha," called Larry Mailliard, slinging his shotgun across his shoulder. "Sounds like a war over here."

— *The New York Times*, November 6, 2008

In busted boomtowns, ministers seek troubled souls

He wore a hat. It was 95 degrees and swampy in South Georgia that October—T-shirt weather—but Michael Brick was wearing a black fedora, not to mention a white long-sleeve button-down and a vest. That was my first inkling: things were about to get interesting. I'd been invited to attend the Auburn Chautauqua, an annual writers gathering, organized and beloved by many of the people in these pages, that takes place over a weekend in the small town of Ludowici. I didn't know any of the people attending that year, 2014, so upon arrival I set about sizing them up. Who were all these guys? (Yes, after two other women canceled, it was 11 guys and me). Brick stood out. He tended to stand when others sat, to hover on the edge of the conversation, listening. When we set about discussing each other's work, he never spoke first. But when he did weigh in, he offered both synthesis and surgical insight. In a group of people who loved to talk about words, he seemed to love words the most. He had kind eyes. He understood that humor was often the best route to empathy, but that sometimes you have to take a hard shot. He enjoyed the power of a parenthetical aside. Shitty writing (and the increasingly draconian economics of our industry) made him mad.

When the weekend was over (we were assigned to read his Kindle single "The Big Race," about a hilarious and insane transcontinental motorcycle ride, but there was also much fond reference to his decade-old New York Times story on Todd Fatjo— if memory serves, some time before or after the leg wrestling, someone read it aloud), I returned to L.A. and went straight down a Brick rabbit hole. His stories remind me of Joseph Mitchell in the way they celebrate the weirdness and originality of regular people. He doesn't pander. He listens to, and then captures, real voices. But to that he adds this: He has the spine to step back and boldly say what's up. "Love is a funny thing," he wrote in that piece on Fatjo (whom he called a "tiny bell-wether" of change in Williamsburg). "It can spin a cynical hipster around like a record (baby, right round, round, round)." Brick loves words. And it shows.

—Amy Wallace

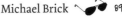

DATELINE: Gonzales, Texas

Maybe God knew the price of crude oil would fall so far so fast. Across Texas, drilling rigs would come down. The bust would leave behind disposal wells and empty hotels, ruined roads and men with no place to go.

God was the one, Hollas Hoffman says, who called him out of retirement at the height of the boom, not even two years ago, to take up a new ministry in the oil fields. God sent him to address early morning safety meetings, to hand out his phone number and most of all to lend an ear in times of grief, addiction and loneliness. God told him, hale at the age of 70, to spread the good news of Jesus Christ to the transient workers of the Eagle Ford Shale.

And God, as layoffs accelerate, has not given any clear order to stop.

"The telephone calls have increased," Hoffman said. "As they lose their jobs, we get calls. I get calls from people who just want to talk. You can tell they're crying. I get calls from wives, I get calls from men. Marriage breakups are fairly common. We've had suicidal calls. We just try to respond to whatever they call about."

From the border to this small town 75 miles east of San Antonio, across the Permian Basin and up through the Panhandle, fading rural churches once hoped to replenish their pews with the arrival of thousands of roughnecks, tool pushers and middle managers, especially those with families in tow. But while some counted an increase in tithing as members leased their land for petroleum extraction, most of the aged congregations gained little in the way of new membership.

"There's kind of a cultural disconnect between the quote-unquote 'oil trash' and the community, the itinerant versus stationary groups," said Andrew Fiser, an earnest young reverend dispatched to coordinate efforts across South Texas for the United Methodist Church. "We really struggled to find the faith communities and specifically lay people that were able to do that work."

The failure of those efforts came as little surprise to Hoffman, who spent four decades as the pastor of half a dozen churches in small towns across the state. He knew firsthand not just the limitations of the pulpit, but also the power of ministry and the audacity required.

Though his parents were, by his description, "not Christian," Hoffman started attending church at the age of 5, when a Sunday school teacher came to fetch him. At first he was confused by talk of the Lord, which he mistook as a reference to the crock jar of pig fat in his grandmother's kitchen, but before long he was singing in the choir. He accepted his savior at age 13. Years of restlessness as a young man led to the righteous path, which eventually led to his retirement career.

Among his qualifications for the ministry, Hoffman counts a gift for easy conversation and the love of his wife, Nelda, who has a better memory for names and other meaningful details. They married as widow and widower. They live in a neighborhood where the streets are named for saints. They wear matching black shirts depicting a derrick and the name of their ministry, Oil Patch Chapel.

"We felt a real need to go out there, and we didn't know exactly why," Hoffman said. "The churches weren't reaching them, so we decided to take the churches to them."

Formally endorsed by the Baptist General Convention of Texas, their work has drawn enough financial support to provide an annual budget of $115,000. Across the state, they have recruited about 60 volunteer chaplains, whom they supply with Bibles, business cards, ministry logo shirts and magnetic car signs. Before the industry layoffs began, they commissioned 4-foot by 48-foot banners that say "Welcome Oil Field Workers," in the hopes that civic leaders might hang them across the highways to foster boomtown goodwill.

Though Hoffman seeks permission from drilling bosses to speak at morning safety meetings, the cards he leaves behind are not primarily intended for managers. Many of those men and women live with their families in comfortable corporate housing. Some of them find churches on their own.

His cards are for the laborers. He encourages them to call in moments of desperation, after accidents and explosions, after bar fights and bouts of boredom, after bad news from home and now, more and more, after layoffs.

"People are distressed, and they don't feel like they have any hope," Hoffman said. "We introduce them to Jesus, and that makes a difference in their lives."

Hoffman likes to call his ministry "a series of interruptions."

Nothing happens on a set schedule. The men he serves live in trailers far from their families, overworked and overpaid, spending their wages on beer and gouged rent. It can be hard to save for a rainy day when the monthly cost of a trailer with four other men exceeds $6,000. Fourteen hour shifts leave little time for making contingency plans. And for those who lose their jobs, oil field work comes with no guarantee of severance pay.

Through charitable donations, Hoffman tries to provide a sort of token safety net. Other than referrals to financial counseling, he can offer little more than a casserole and perhaps a small grocery store gift card.

But the most important contribution he and his wife make to troubled workers is "their love," said Rebecca Salmon, whose husband broke his neck driving an oil field truck. "They share their love with you."

Reaching those workers, especially in times of distress, presents an enduring challenge. One of his volunteer chaplains, Stan Hays, a pipeline construction supervisor, struggled for years to spread a gospel message in the oil fields before signing on with Hoffman.

"The guys I call 'hard-core criminals,' out of prison, struggling in their lives, they don't want to hear it from me," Hays said. "They think I'm fake."

Hoffman takes a gentle approach. His advanced age, he says, helps put men at ease. His choice of the title "chaplain" suggests he does not intend to cajole anyone into church attendance.

At a construction site for a disposal facility outside town the other day, Hoffman struck up a conversation with Alan Gao, 31, an operations coordinator for the oil field waste management firm Trisun Energy. They talked about the price of crude. Hoffman said he was planning to attend a speech by the chairman of the Railroad Commission, which regulates the oil industry. Maybe, he suggested, he could return with some insights about business conditions.

After the small talk ran out, Hoffman made a pitch for his ministry.

"When we try to help your workers, or you, we never interfere with their work schedule," he said. "If you have somebody that's in distress, they're probably not going to be as good a worker. So please feel free to call on us. We have people that can be there in 20 minutes if you have a wreck or an explosion."

Hoffman was not the first to hear a calling to the oil fields. After the discovery of hydrocarbons around Crane County in 1926, a real estate developer named O.C. Kinnison invited a preacher to bring some perspective to the descending mobs. In the 1940s, an oil speculator named Rupert Ricker held tent revival meetings in Big Spring.

Nearly a quarter century ago, the Oilfield Christian Fellowship of Houston started printing scriptures customized with petroleum industry testimonials.

But the latest boom descended on a vastly altered state, where oil field operations take their orders from corporate towers in the populous urban triangle of Houston, Dallas and San Antonio. Many established churches in the far-flung oil fields were already struggling.

"The first thought was, 'Let's offer them coffee and muffins,' " said Valli Blair, pastor of Three Rivers United Methodist Church. "But that isn't what they need. They need AA. They need to know about their health. They need to know how to support their family in their absence."

In Carrizo Springs, where Pastor Vanessa LeVine took office last summer at the United Methodist Church, there has been talk of using the windfall from industry royalty checks to hire a paid outreach director. As oil production companies order more layoffs and transfers, though, she can hardly see the point.

"We have one family with two beautiful children," she said. "The wife was going to help with the Christmas pageant. No sooner did she sign up than did her husband get put on alert that he might have to move to West Texas at any time."

For the ministry of Hollas and Nelda Hoffman, though, rebuilding congregations ranks as a secondary concern at best.

One day last week, Hoffman returned to the home of the trucker who had broken his neck, John Salmon, known around the fleet yard as Stretch. He was still in a neck brace, but he was up walking around, shooing the chickens in his yard and the dogs in his living room.

After an exchange of pleasantries, Hoffman asked about surgery schedules. Salmon said little; his wife and his mother and the other women in the house did most of the talking. A date in the spring was mentioned, though all present agreed that his recovery was in the hands of God.

"We're going to have a prayer with you, if that's okay, and then we're going to get down the road," Hoffman said. The women bowed their heads. Salmon could not, but he closed his eyes. "Father," Hoffman prayed, "thank you for your healing hand. We ask that you be with us as we go out and minister to others. We thank you for healing John. In Jesus' name, Amen."

"Amen," said everybody.

Then Hoffman got on down the road. Over chicken fried steaks in the dining room of the local auction barn, he chatted up the communal table and offered a prayer. Then he drove out through fields of pumpjacks and grazing cattle, down rutted dirt roads past empty well pad sites and rows of abandoned mobile home hookups. He kept his phone close, and when it rang he felt compelled to answer the call.

—*The Houston Chronicle*, February 8, 2015

Longhorn, Sooner fans experience different twist to weekend revelry

So here was Mike Brick back in '93, in Dallas, in the drunk tank—as a reporter or a detainee, it's not clear. In college journalism, you don't care so much about crossing those lines.

It was the weekend of the Texas-Oklahoma football game at the Cotton Bowl, and while other student journalists dutifully chronicled the game (Sooners 38, Longhorns 17), Brick somehow got himself into the Dallas PD detox cell and took notes.

He was—what? 19—but he knew what to look for. The vomiting-and-urine hole, the Vietnam vet putting the Gulf War grunt in his place, the student determined to call his lawyer daddy: Details and characters like these would animate Brick's writing for years to come.

What gets me most, though, is the way Brick suspends judgment. He's a kid, but he's not scandalized; he's not going to moralize about the chilly man shouting "ugly-ass ho" or the guard who replies with a blast of mace. There are no good guys here, and no bad guys. Just guys, fucking up and sobering up and surrendering to sleep.

As an editor, I try to encourage this kind of this restraint in writers, with middling success. They like to explain, usually with adjectives. Michael Brick, of The Daily Texan, understood that you explain best by not explaining.

—Mike Wilson

DATELINE: Dallas, Texas

Finally, they all went to sleep.

After hours of screaming, picking fights, hogging mattress pads and making idle threats at guards, the more than 30 drunks, rowdies and bystanders in Male Dorm B of the Dallas Police Department's detox center either passed out or took to staring at the wall.

Joining the crowd of regulars in the drunk tank Friday night was an assortment of Longhorn and Sooner fans, many of whom had driven hours for the experience.

And because they were charged with public intoxication, a misdemeanor based on whether the arresting officer believes the suspect is intoxicated, they went to jail in varying states of sobriety.

Police are not required to read Miranda rights to public intoxication suspects, or to test their blood-alcohol levels. For the Texas-OU weekend crackdown, police used strips of plastic as handcuffs, and loaded the drunken revelers into paddywagons.

Between 1 and 2 a.m., the football fans began to enter the detox center in full force. A group of five college students, one wearing a Texas T-shirt and the other four singing Oklahoma fight songs, were brought in around 2 a.m.

After being stripped of their belts, wallets, keys and other potential weapons, they were escorted from the approximately 8-by-10-foot holding tank—complete with a vomiting and urine hole—to the larger detox room to sober up.

The student with the UT shirt immediately headed for one of the hard blue pads to sleep, while the others set to picking fights.

Just about anything qualified as a reason to fight, including the obvious: "Shit, man, I bet you're from Oklahoma."

One Sooner fan complained loudly that he had fought in the Persian Gulf and therefore did not belong in jail.

"Sit your Desert Storm ass down. I was in Vietnam," said an older man, stalking across the room toward the Sooner fan.

As the shoving began, a guard came into the room, grabbed two of the Sooner fans, and dragged them out. A UT Arlington student, displaying large welts from the plastic handcuffs, approached everyone who seemed at least mildly coherent to ask for their names and phone numbers.

"You can tell I'm not drunk, can't you," he said. "My dad's a lawyer in Connecticut... I'm going to get out of this."

Around 5 a.m., one man began a tirade against the guards that lasted more than an hour, demanding they turn off the air conditioning.

"Hey, ugly-ass ho," he screamed. "Y'all got coats out there and you're freezing me. Y'all better give us some jackets, ugly-ass ho. Hey, ugly-ass ho."

After nearly half an hour, the guard opened the door, sprayed mace into the room and left again.

By 6 a.m., the relatively sober began to realize they could be bailed out, and began to demand telephone calls, pantomiming telephone conversations to the guards through a plexiglass window.

After friends—and in some cases parents—shelled out $110 bail to free the students, they hit the streets again, most with enough time for a nap before the football game.

— *The Daily Texan*, October 11, 1993

Austin's Franklin Barbecue is All the Rage, and Long Lines are a Daily Ritual

Franklin Barbecue is a place where hopeful fanatics wait in line for hours, knowing from the start that once they get to the front they might learn it was all for naught. That's the setting for this dispatch: the surprising new Mecca of meat culture.

A lesser writer—the vast majority of writers—would find that interesting enough, and this would be a one-off fad story about the hottest new joint in town. But this story is about much more than the hundreds of pounds of brisket and pork passing through the smokers every day. It's about people: the young upstart taking his place among the greats, the veteran counterparts living in a new world, the fetishists and ubiquitous bloggers. It's about the history and geography, with a first sentence that places us both physically and culturally. And, like so many other great Michael Brick stories, it's about gentrification: the whitening of Austin, Texas.

Fans of fine writing will also notice the deft storytelling, the understated humor, the perfect pacing. Reading it feels like listening to someone sitting around a fire. His characters are sharp and witty, and the writer has obvious affection for them. Wonderful phrases like "approximately all" and "at full whirl" and "the now-ceremonious Running Out of the Meat" are marbled into the prose so as to flavor but never distract from the tale itself.

And in the end, the reader is left satiated and pleased, but longing for the next chance to consume a piece of writing so good.

—Michael Mooney

DATELINE: Austin, Texas

Outside a one-room hillside shack on East 11th Street, under an archway greeting visitors to the state's first African American Cultural Heritage District, the people wait to eat. Among those who ascribe transcendent qualities to the production of barbecue—there are surprisingly many, approximately all with their own blogs—the waiting has become a daily ritual.

True to the butcher paper sign affixed to its entrance, Franklin Barbecue operates at full whirl for about an hour and 20 minutes a day—serving 600 pounds of brisket, ribs, pulled pork, sausage and a sandwich called the Tipsy Texan—"til the meat runs out," at which point a companionable worker named John Avila turns away dozens of unblessed patrons.

For a marketing ploy, the new restaurant could do worse, though its proprietors emphatically deny any such agency in the now-ceremonious Running Out of the Meat.

"If we could make more and maintain the same quality," Avila says every afternoon, with some variation and usually a shrug, "we would totally do it."

Witnesses to the quality of the brisket—a juicy, crusted specimen bathed in ketchup, cider vinegar and coffee—include *Garden & Gun* magazine, *Food & Wine* magazine and bloggers galore.

"This," testified Daniel Vaughn, a Dallas critic who blogs at the site Full Custom Gospel BBQ, "is nothing short of the best brisket in Texas."

* * *

The location once housed Ben's Long Branch, the front dining room of black East Austin.

While rival Sam's BBQ up on East 12th Street served mostly neighborhood regulars, solemn-faced foodies and Stevie Ray Vaughan, Ben's Long Branch made a point of bridging the divide to establishment Austin. Its owner, Ben Wash, still speaks fondly of Mack Brown, Ron Kirk and Rick Perry, politics aside.

Barbecue occupies a curious position on the cultural land-scape. No other comfort food inspires such one-upmanship and interregional grudge-holding. There's something deeply primal about standing over a fire pit, dominating and babying a slab of meat. It's been thoroughly fetishized, with complex rules concerning where to stand, how long to wait and whether to apply sauce—and those are just for the eaters.

Then there's the race thing, inescapable for any invention of the rural South. To oversimplify: Either you worry about driving into a given part of town to eat barbecue, or about stopping in a given county. The fear you feel confirms what's known as authenticity.

Few pitmasters have worked this angle more expertly than Ben Wash. In 1996, for example, a black competitor named John Goode lost his subcontract to serve brisket at city-owned venues after refusing to register as a minority-owned business. To comply with Austin's affirmative action policy, the main contractor hired—who else?—Ben's Long Branch.

By then, the ground was shifting on East 11th. A decade and tens of millions of dollars later, the block has been rebranded as the East End Independent Business Investment Zone, where a mural depicting black horn players leads to bistros, condos and galleries full of white faces.

"It's nothing strange to me," Wash says. "There's just not many of us here. It's not like Dallas or Houston. I did well here. I'd guess my business was 85 or 90 percent white. I don't think nothing of it. It's been going this way for years."

Three years ago, Wash retired, leasing the building to "some white guys who hired a manager from Connecticut."

"This guy didn't know what he was doing," Wash says, "and I told him he didn't know what he was doing."

The arrangement did not last long. Even at 71, Wash has never stopped cooking. (Attention bloggers: He still serves brisket from a trailer by a country road two or three days a week—happy hunting!) But without a family successor, he started looking for a serious contender to take over the lease.

* * *

Texas barbecue, a subcategory or a separate one depending on whom you ask, builds partisanship the same way baseball does: Powerhouse dynasties like Kreuz Market, Sonny Bryan's and Angelo's dominate for decades, hardening positions on all sides.

But in recent years, a sense of uncertainty has crept into the field. Not uncertainty exactly —possibility, call it. In 2008, the state's leading generator of lists, *Texas Monthly* magazine, declared the previously obscure Snow's of Lexington its No. 1 barbecue restaurant. Much consternation ensued. Bloggers blogged it from hell to breakfast. Eventually, it became necessary for *New Yorker* correspondent Calvin Trillin to come see what was what.

Into the breach rode young Aaron Franklin, a musician, restaurant worker and backyard grilling hobbyist, who made his professional debut from a camper parked behind a friend's coffee shop. He served three briskets, cutting the meat, operating the register, washing his hands and repeating the process. Bloggers got on the case ricky-tick. In March 2010, South by Southwest invited Franklin to a barbecue showcase (the festival has expanded considerably beyond its musical origins).

"Somehow, I totally nudged my way into that," Franklin said, "some scrawny white kid trying to make barbecue with the old-timers."

Now 33, Franklin does cut a dubious profile for a pitmaster. "Scrawny white kid" fails to fully capture his aspect. Plenty of Austin hipsters wear Elvis sideburns and vintage G.I.-style glasses, but how many can say they played drums in an indie rock band (Those Peabodys) that managed, without ever scoring a major label deal, to inspire its own devoted cover band (Bros Peabodys)?

But Franklin put in the hours. He started work at 4 a.m. He welded the smoker by hand. He scoffed at any fuel source but wood. He spread the meat widely across the grill (providing a plausible explanation for the daily running-out routine).

"Spending the time to make it good," Franklin said. "That's what it comes down to."

* * *

By the end of the year, lines to his camper stretched down the block. Franklin went looking for a roof. He found Ben Wash, whose mother did not raise a fool. Just before Christmas, the two men agreed to a long-term lease.

Franklin ripped out the smokers, rebuilt the dining room and painted the facade aquamarine. The former home of the Long Branch became a fit house of barbecue once again, though some never knew the difference.

"I never was around when that other joint was open," said Brad Istre, 33, a graphic designer from Mesquite (his blog: ManUpTexasBBQ). "But I would say it kind of goes with the gentrification that's going on in East Austin."

Of course, Franklin was no pioneer. His restaurant was preceded into the neighborhood by a purveyor of green laundry products, a "work/life balance & wellness center" and a bistro where the management strives (and says so right on the menu) for "a sense of purpose and meaning beyond our basic financial goals."

But this is barbecue. Meaningful food. Sam's, still thriving on East 12th, welcomed the competition — sort of.

"He's got to know about the history of the community," said Bill Green, a cook at Sam's. "Being new, moving into this neighborhood, from a business standpoint, maybe that's all he needs. But I know the person that owned that place before Ben owned it. My dad drove a cab in Austin, Texas, for 35 years. I wish everyone that opens a business on the Eastside good luck, because this pie's big enough for all of us, but when you're moving into a neighborhood that's full of history, you've got to get to know the community. Of course, that's just my opinion."

There was a time, before he moved into the old Long Branch, when Franklin could take a joke about the severity of his whiteness. "My last name's Franklin," he once conceded, "so maybe that fools people into thinking there's an old black guy out here."

* * *

But now the pressure is on. Rent is due. He's bought two 20-foot shipping containers to outfit as brick grill pits, with designs on serving

1,800 pounds of meat a day. He's adding bathrooms. He's contemplating a beer garden.

As he expounded on these ambitions, Franklin shrugged off questions of black and white, carefully shifting the subject to age. "That just goes with the diversity of barbecue," he said. "Some young white whippersnapper under 60 trying to do barbecue, an old man's game. It attracts all kinds."

The sold-out sign was up. The dining room was clearing out. Franklin turned the conversation to traditions he holds dear, matters of meat and fire. On East 11th Street, he said, his craft has found a home.

"I think the neighborhood reception's been super-awesome," he said. "Hopefully we'll be here for a long time, and become an institution."

—*The Dallas Morning News,* June 8, 2011

PART THREE: OCCURRENCES

Night That Girl, 7, Died Is Recounted in Family Court

Toiling in the trenches of daily news for a big-city paper is an efficient way to acquaint yourself with the very worst that humanity and random fate have to offer.

Some stories Mike wrote: "Disabled Girl Is Found Dead In Trash Truck." "Father Is Accused of Hanging Toddler at a Queens Motel." "Homeless Man Is Crushed By Trash-Lifter."

There was never a shortage of disheartening happenings in Brooklyn, where Mike and I worked side by side for three years on the 25th floor of a dingy, leaky office building filled with ambulance-chasing lawyers, our desks commanding sweeping views of the Verrazano-Narrows Bridge and the green infinity of Staten Island, the drop-ceiling tiles above us perpetually bursting with brown water and raining chunks into hastily placed trash cans.

And for sheer, heartbreaking awfulness and evil, there was nothing like the case of Nixzmary Brown, a big-eyed girl abused and starved for years by her mother and stepfather until finally, at the age of 7, she committed the capital offense of taking a treat from the refrigerator without permission—initially said to be yogurt, later corrected to pudding—and was beaten and thrown in a tub to die.

On a Tuesday in October 2006, Mike reported to family court, where a hearing was being held for the absurd-sounding purpose of allowing a judge to discern whether Nixzmary's stepfather, Cesar Rodriguez, in jail and awaiting trial for her murder, was fit to take custody of her surviving siblings.

At the hearing, the tape of Mr. Rodriguez's statement to a prosecutor was played.

Mike let the facts, and Mr. Rodriguez's words, speak for themselves.

—Andy Newman

DATELINE: Brooklyn, New York

Cesar Rodriguez turned in his chair and waited for the image of Cesar Rodriguez to appear on the courtroom wall. He sat there beside his translator and his wife and their lawyers and his extended family and their lawyers and translators and the city lawyers and the court officers who had handguns.

He had come to this civil proceeding yesterday from jail, where he and his wife, Nixzaliz Santiago, await trial on murder charges in the death of her 7-year-old daughter, Nixzmary Brown. Although one of Nixzmary's four brothers is in the custody of his biological father, it has fallen to Judge Nora L. Freeman of Brooklyn Family Court to determine who is fit to raise the other three brothers and a sister, none older than 10, and all in the custody of the city's child welfare agency.

To show that the answer is not Cesar Rodriguez, city lawyers played a videotape of his statement to an assistant district attorney, Linda Weinman. The image of Mr. Rodriguez appeared on the wall, and the live Mr. Rodriguez watched this simulacrum, both of them turned and leaning and poker-faced. In the image, his hands were clasped. He sat next to a clock with a sweeping second hand that went around and around so the police could show that the recording had not been altered.

Ms. Weinman asked Mr. Rodriguez to tell her what had happened the night Nixzmary was killed, Jan. 10. He said, "I don't know where to begin."

Then he spoke of a shopping trip, of returning to their Bedford-Stuyvesant home and distributing yogurt to reward good behavior, of Nixzmary's exclusion from this treat. He listed flavors, berries and cream and chocolate. Nixzmary, he said, was in a back room with the cat box and some mattresses, a chair and a rope on the door. He had been restraining her there, he said, "by putting duct tape on her hands and tying her to the chair."

Mr. Rodriguez said Nixzmary had been misbehaving since before Christmas, beating up her four brothers and one sister and telling him lies.

"Sometimes she used to get me real angry," Mr. Rodriguez said, "and I used to just throw her."

Throw her where, he was asked.

"On the floor."

Things would go missing in the apartment, things would get broken, Mr. Rodriguez said, and always the other children would blame Nixzmary and he would believe them and Nixzmary would lie.

Ms. Weinman said, "Why do you think she's lying to you?"

Mr. Rodriguez said, "Because she's always lying to me."

That night, he said, yogurt vanished and computer gear was broken and again Nixzmary lied and he threatened her with a belt. He said he asked her to explain but she only nodded. Nodded how, he was asked.

"Like this," Mr. Rodriguez said, "like she doesn't know what's going on."

He said he threw cold water on her and dunked her head in the bathtub. Ms. Weinman showed him pictures of her injuries. In the pictures the girl was lifeless and skeletal. Her eyes and nose and chin looked like black flowers, dark abrasions circled her ankle, and her back was pounded to tenders. The judge ordered the tape stopped. In the courtroom, Ms. Santiago was sobbing.

"Mi hija," she cried, and the court officers brought tissues.

The tape resumed: Mr. Rodriguez said Nixzmary's black eyes had been self-inflicted. He said his wife had found Nixzmary alive after the last beating. He could tell because she was making a noise, he said. The prosecutor asked him to describe this noise.

"Like when you have a pain," Mr. Rodriguez said, "and you just go, 'Ohwwwwwwwwwwwhn.'"

— *The New York Times*, October 18, 2006

Undercover Agent
in Real Fur Snares a
Fake Veterinarian

Down in south Georgia every fall, the writer Thomas Lake brings together a group of writers at his family place near Ludowici, a spot on the map that once held the distinction of being the most notorious speed trap in the state. It is not far from the Atlantic and not far from the Okefenokee. A 300-year-old live oak stands guard at the back door. Mosquitoes weigh about a pound. Little wild kittens tussle in the shrubbery, and out back a glorified screen porch doubles as a party house. Inside, world-class writers tussle, intellectually and sometimes, when spirits run high, physically. These wordsmiths spend their lives otherwise writing articles and books and winning awards. At Ludowici, they lovingly contest one another to see who will, someday, some way, write the best thing ever written.

After a day of readings and sometimes-contentious discussions, writers break out musical instruments, and the roof of the party house jumps up and down like something in a Saturday morning cartoon. A true thing in life is that most writers want to be musicians, and most musicians want to be writers.

The first trip I made to Ludowici a few years ago, the after-hours caterwauling went on and on. Several stump-the-band guitarists and a dozen other folks who knew words and music and, sometimes, entire catalogues, sang till voices went hoarse, brave dead-soldier beer bottles lined the walls, and broken picks littered the floor.

Deep in the night, all the Drive-By Truckers and Cat Stevens and Steve Earle and Paul Simon and Hank and Patsy and Neil Young and even the Cokesbury hymns sent up like sparks to the sky, the guitars took a break.

And something happened.

Michael Brick picked up my Martin. He strummed a warm-up chord, and then quietly, impeccably, played two of his own songs.

An angel came down. The crazy cabin hushed. The night changed.

I wish Michael Brick lived next door to me. I wish I could slip through a hedge and ease up onto his porch to hear him play those two songs of his own creation.

I wish I could pray the way those songs did.

I would pray Michael back, to play his tunes for us.

—Charles McNair

DATELINE: New York, New York

The place was New York City. Crime was the dish of the day, and the main course was injury to an animal with a side of petty larceny. The victim was Burt. Burt was a Boston terrier. He was about to find a friend who looked more like a foe.

The case unraveled over six months, with an indictment this week. The details spilled from court documents and interviews with investigators and Burt's owner, Raymond Reid.

For four years, Burt had been under the care of Steven Vassall, 28, an unemployed lab technician who styled himself a licensed veterinarian. Mr. Vassall gave Burt vaccinations and heartworm treatments and sometimes boarded him. Mr. Reid liked Mr. Vassall. Mr. Vassall made house calls.

Mr. Reid left for vacation in August, but he got an urgent call from Mr. Vassall. Burt was in a bad way. Burt had swallowed a foreign object. Burt was going to die.

Mr. Reid came home and said he wanted to see Burt. Mr. Vassall let Burt out of the car and drove away. Burt had an open wound along his abdomen, and he was licking the blood.

Mr. Vassall sent Mr. Reid a bill for $985. Mr. Reid called the Brooklyn district attorney.

The district attorney, Charles J. Hynes, put his top investigators on the case. Rackets Division. Senior people. A sting was arranged. An apartment was wired. But this mousetrap was all spring and no cheese.

Carol Moran was working a steady 9 to 5 in the district attorney's office. She had 22 years on the job. For this case, she was going to need a sidekick. That's where Fred came in.

Fred was the strong, silent type with no place to come in out of the rain. He was an alley cat from the streets of Brooklyn, long and lean with thick black stripes. Ms. Moran took a shine to him right away. She adopted him from Animal Care and Control.

Fred never asked to be a hero, but he needed work. And neutering. Mr. Vassall agreed to end Fred's sex life for $135. Last Friday, he picked up Fred and the payment. Fred was in a carrying case. The payment was in cash.

Mr. Vassall was charged with unauthorized veterinary practice, criminal mischief, injuring animals and petty larceny. He was free on bail but could not be reached; his phone was disconnected. His lawyer, Royce Russell, declined to comment.

The victim was stitched up. The hero wore a badge to meet the news media. His big green eyes looked past a dozen TV cameras. A dozen camera operators made kissy noises.

A tabloid reporter asked the district attorney a tabloid question.

"This is the first, Nance," Mr. Hynes said. "First undercover cat."

Then Fred took a nap in the corner. Tomorrow was another day. His owner said neutering was still in the works.

—*The New York Times*, February 9, 2006

Sorority of the Swamp

Mike Brick's second phone call to me came just as I was beginning to forget him. And I couldn't help but be amazed at his perfect timing. It was the late 1990s, and Mike had first called me a number of weeks before. He said that he was looking to land a job as a researcher for a book author, and someone had told him to call me at The New York Times, where I worked as a reporter. Mike told me he worked in the press office of a Texas state legislator and had also previously done some reporting for the Austin American-Statesman. While I was just starting my book "The Informant", nothing about Mike's background suggested he would be the right person for a researcher job. I had no positions available at that point, I told him. I recommended that he call me back in the future to see if I was ready to hire somebody.

Mike didn't know that this was a test. A key part of reporting was knowing how to hit that sweet spot where you avoid harassing people while making sure they remember you. Mike's second call was right in the sweet spot. As was the third. And the fourth. While his resume did not suggest he was qualified for the job, his persistence and smarts left me impressed. I told him I would meet with him if he ever came up to New York from Austin. I told him not to make a special trip, but he did anyway. If I remember correctly, he slept on a friend's floor in Manhattan.

We had lunch at a pizza place just off Times Square. By the end of our conversation, I knew that Mike was very green when it came to journalism, a little bit prone to conspiracy theories, but incredibly eager. Something told me I should ignore his resume and instead focus on his character. I think I hired him that day, and I told him a few things: I didn't expect researchers to be perfect, but making the same mistake repeatedly could result in him *being fired. In fact, I had fired a number of researchers in the past. The pay was dreadful, I told him, but I adopted the careers of every researcher who performed well. If he succeeded, I told Mike, I would help him professionally for as long as he wanted my assistance.*

Mike moved to New York and I gave him his first assignment. I believe it involved having him travel to Illinois to conduct some reporting. He wrote a memo and attached documents he had located. And his work... sucked. What he provided was almost useless; he hadn't answered the question I had asked and had veered off on another topic. I sat down with Mike and reviewed everything he had done and explained the errors he had made. I assumed I would be firing him soon. In my experience, few researchers could improve as much as Mike needed to. Still, I gave him another chance and another assignment. (But just in case he didn't work out, I hired a second researcher with a stronger background in journalism to pick up the slack.)

When Mike finished his reporting, he delivered his second memo, and it was again loaded with mistakes. But I noticed that he repeated none of the errors from his first assignment. I spoke with him again about what he had done wrong. It was then I noticed something unusual: Mike was soaking up every word. There was no dismay in his eyes at being told his work was insufficient; instead, everything I saw just told me he wanted to get better.

The third assignment came back; once again, while there were flaws, all of them were errors that had never appeared before. Everything we had previously discussed as problems simply disappeared. We spoke again. I became awed at how fast Mike learned. He and I began to have very long conversations about journalism, sometimes as they related to an assignment and sometimes just because there were things I thought he should know. The transformation was amazing to watch. This once-poorly qualified, inexperienced reporter was becoming a talented journalist before my eyes.

Eventually, my research needs for "The Informant" ended, and by then Mike was amazing. His reporting was top-notch. He was a better writer than me. The student had surpassed the teacher. I told Mike that, not only was I adopting his career, but I was going to get him a job at The New York Times.

I spoke with Jack Lynch, an editor at the Times *who oversaw what was then the joint newsroom between the newspaper and its recent acquisition, thestreet.com. I told him this story and said that, while I had hired* many researchers in the past, Mike was far and away the best. This was an amazing fact, I told Jack, because he had started as the worst. Give this kid a shot and there was no telling how far he would go. Jack met with Mike and I guess he saw the same thing in him that I did. He hired Mike for a reporter's job. (Not a lot of time passed before other Times editors recognized the amazing things that make Mike the person he is. He was hired full-time as a Times reporter.)

While Mike was still working in the joint newsroom, "The Informant" was published. In the acknowledgments, along with the usual recitations of gratitude, I wrote about Mike. Remember his name, I wrote. He will "do big things in journalism." Once again, I underestimated him. Yes, he did big things in journalism, but he also did so much more. In 2002, he and I worked together reporting and writing for the Times about Enron. Then he became an author, writing his own books, including the tour de force "Saving the School." I read that book awed once again by Mike's never-ending upward trajectory. Soon, he was a husband and a father, and he always spoke glowingly of his family.

I still hire researchers, and whenever I do, I tell them this story about the young man who became a marvel by dint of his commitment and refusal to quit. I am honored to say that Mike Brick is my friend. I admire him more than I can say for everything he has done in his life.

He is one of the most remarkable people I have ever known.

—Kurt Eichenwald

DATELINE: Sherard, Mississippi

The leader of the hunting party carried a 12-gauge Winchester 101 repeating shotgun with a wooden stock. Standing thigh-deep in the stagnant bottoms of Willow Hole, where a Labrador retriever named Congo whimpered from a twilit hardwood's bend, she waited for first shooting light, the moment a half-hour before sunrise when hunters can legally fire on the wood ducks gliding overhead.

"Is it time yet?" whispered one of the group's hunters, Kate Morrison, 45, from Memphis, a stay-at-home mother of two boys.

"About one minute," said the leader, Allison Crews, 42, an owner of a small insurance company in Canton, Miss.

They call themselves the Swamp Witches, a half-dozen women pledged to return twice a year to the Ward Lake Hunting Club, a privately owned 6,500-acre conservation parcel here in the floodplain of the Mississippi Delta. Hard by the Arkansas border, some 140 miles northwest of Jackson, the club occupies a prime span of the Mississippi Flyway, migratory route to generations of waterfowl and one of the most widely envied birding grounds in North America.

In recent years, nonprofit groups have sought to expand the appeal of duck hunting among women, sponsoring clinics from Colusa County, Calif., to Cape Girardeau, Mo. Eager to broaden their market, outfitters like Avery Outdoors have provided free gear.

But so far, women have remained in the distinct minority. Of the 244,000 Mississippians who went hunting in 2006, the year of the most recent survey by the United States Fish and Wildlife Service, only about 30,000 were women. Nationally, women accounted for 6 percent of all migratory bird hunters, a decline from 186,000 in 1996 to 131,000 in 2006. Merely by hunting outside the company of their fathers, husbands, brothers and sons, the Swamp Witches made for an unusual sight, said Tony Dolle, spokesman for Ducks Unlimited, a wetlands conservation outfit based in Memphis.

Bound by an informal sorority of the outdoors, the Swamp Witches embrace some antiquated ways. At a time when many hunters have grown accustomed to driving or motor boating to their duck blinds, these women prefer to feel the ooze of the muck below their boots, to propel their canoes by their own muscle, to inhale the pungent methane of the marsh, to wade its unknowable waters.

"It's not very common for that to happen in that form," Dolle said. "I don't know if I'd call it old-fashioned. The methodology that they use is older and more traditional. It can be tougher hunting."

Accountings of the group's origins were confused, in dispute or both. The women keep no archivist, no historian, though they have been known to employ a chef. Most agreed that they came together more than a decade ago through a shared passion for horseback riding.

Their leader, Crews, is the wife of a prominent lawyer in Madison County. Her father-in-law, James M. Crews Jr., had spent decades acquiring the land around Ward Lake for conservation and private hunting by a club of 33 families. In one telling, James M. Crews III had first called the women Swamp Witches in honor of their zeal.

The relating of this history—told over red wine in a cabin decorated with a state flag, a topographical map, duck decoys, family pictures and a bookshelf full of war memoirs—was interrupted just before supper one Sunday last month for a prayer.

As the party dined on shrimp 'n' grits, duck Wellington (the chef, Chris Robinson of Memphis, had reduced the gaminess of the meat with a marinade of milk) and tiramisu, the women recounted their first hunting excursions. Susan Williams, 52, an importer from Clinton, spoke of a pride so deep that she had felt inspired to show off her first slain duck, in frozen form, at a New Year's Eve party.

"That's a validation for the women," Williams said. "A lot of people say, 'Oh, sure, women hunt, but there are men putting out the decoys for them.' We have our own dogs, we put out our own decoys, we do it all without power, we canoe in."

The group had been subjected to some curious questions over the years—"Do y'all have to have a license, like males do?" one man was said to have asked—but Crews, reserved and proper, struck a more diplomatic tone.

"We're not out to prove anything," she said. "We just like it."

That night the witches bedded down early, expecting a difficult hunt. The next day would be a Monday; stirred by weekend hunters, the ducks would be wary. And with few other hunters out on a weekday, the ducks would have their pick of safe landing places. With all that in mind, Crews had left a bind of slain ducks in the swamp overnight for the group's traditional commemorative photographs. At 4:45 a.m., she rousted her witches with a call of "Morning."

Down the hallway came Morrison; Williams; Lind Bussey, 50, of Jackson; Leigh Bailey, 46, a real estate developer from Clinton; and Lila Sessums, 43, a show horse rider from Clinton. The women pulled on their boots, gathered their weapons and rallied their dogs. From the kitchen, Sessums sang a chorus of "You Never Even Called Me by My Name."

She had a wild look in her eye, this Lila Sessums. Boarding an all-terrain vehicle laden with a bouquet of daisies and an infant car seat, she followed Crews through a clearing under a veiled moon near full. The women sang cackles into the blackness, turning now through a vine-webbed forest of hackberry and cypress, loosing the hounds to run, driving until they came upon the water's edge.

Together they waded into the mire, launched canoes and paddled past beaver holes, buckbrush and cypress knees. At Willow Hole they debarked. Crews set out decoys. She rotated her leg through the water, drawing ripples in imitation of resting ducks. The women hid beneath low-hanging branches around the perimeter. Congo took his place on the aged willow trunk. The distant trees looked like teepees. From one of them a great horned owl called. Wood ducks squealed, too. Then the sky turned acrylic and shotgun reports crumpled the stillness. The women blasted their steel shells skyward and Congo leapt into the chill lake waters, but nothing fell.

"No, Congo," Crews said, guiding the dog back to his perch. "No bird. I know you have faith."

She sounded a duck call, her fingers fluttering over the mouth of the horn as if for a blues harp solo. Four gadwalls responded, circling back over Willow Hole, diving toward the decoys. The women opened fire into the windless sky, aiming for a clean kill as the birds came within perhaps 40 yards. Again the ducks escaped.

"I said to shoot them, not shoot at them," Crews admonished.

Morrison laughed at her own poor aim, saying, "They were too close."

Daylight extended, and frustration too. Hours passed with no ducks in sight. Sessums smoked light cigarettes and threatened passing blackbirds. Somebody poured cream liqueur from a flask. Wagering ensued. Crews and Bussey paddled across the swamp and back again in a luckless effort to scare up a flock. By afternoon the women were due to return to their husbands and their children and their jobs and their social engagements.

In time a large flock soared far, far overhead. Here was one last chance. The women crouched in the swamp and sounded their calls and waited.

"Thirty of them above us," Crews whispered. "Thirty sets of eyes looking down."

But the ducks did not descend. For the women, other obligations were waiting. Crews began to pack the canoes.

"Well, I got the witches here," she said. "The witches are harder to get than the ducks."

Across Willow Hole, Bailey fed the last biscuits from breakfast to the dogs. Morrison touched up her lip gloss. Sessums was still scanning the heavens, shotgun aloft, looking for something to shoot. She sang: "Ducky love, ducky love, come on in, ducky love."

— *The New York Times*, February 5, 2009

The Big Race

On the American Road,
In Pursuit of a Mystery Man, a Film Crew
and a Pack of Bikers
From Arizona to the Pine Ridge Reservation
(With a Brief Interlude in Las Vegas)

Mark Twain wrote two great novels and many profound half-truths, including this semi-Biblical pronouncement on the human condition: "The lack of money is the root of all evil." There is something about Michael Brick's writing that reminds me of Twain, something wry and old-fashioned and hilarious, and I see it most clearly in this story about a cross-country motorcycle race. It's easy to imagine the main character, Big Jim Red Cloud, taking marbles and kites from the boys he has tricked into whitewashing Aunt Polly's fence. But my favorite character in the story is Brick himself, who merrily leads us into the madness of the race while only hinting at his own precarious circumstances. In the aftermath of the Great Recession, as a magazine freelancer with a wife and two young children, Brick had some thin operating margins. He helped finance the trip with a $2,000 line of credit and, as he writes in Part One, "charmed my way through some cashflow-related indignity at the hotel check-in." In the end, lack of money is the root of a great moment in American journalism, a moment worthy of Mark Twain, a moment I will always wish I had witnessed: a former New York Times reporter covering his travel expenses by throwing dice in a discount casino.

—Thomas Lake

Part One

DATELINE: Mesa, Arizona

August 3, 2011

Two days before the race, in the asphalt lot at Chester's Harley-Davidson of Mesa, Arizona, where the temperature measured 108 degrees, Big Jim asked to inspect my driver's license. Refusal was an option, but not a good one. To get my media credentials, I needed to win his favor. Hoisting the card in his ample palm, he made note of my home address, aloud. Then he said, "Good, because if you tell any lies about me, I'm going to come to your house and mess you up."

I slid the license back into my billfold and sized the man up. In two decades as a newspaper reporter, I had come across some tough customers, enough to tell bluster from menace. Big Jim, aka Jim Red Cloud, aka James G. Durham, scanned as an even split. At 56, he stood about 6'5", 260 pounds, with a ruddy complexion and dark spiky hair. He was wearing size-14 flip-flops, camouflage-print shorts, hoop earrings, a sweaty yellow bandanna and Ray-Ban sunglasses tinted red. He was smoking Marlboros. Not Lights, Reds, from a hard pack. His smile and his scowl alternated without intermission.

Big Jim is a white man, but he presents himself as a tireless advocate for the Oglala Sioux, a Lakota faction based on the Pine Ridge Reservation in North Dakota. His admirers say he can prophesy death, diagnose asymptomatic disease and ascertain a man's position on the path toward enlightenment. His detractors call him a bully, a charlatan and worse. He had come to the desert to stage the boldest undertaking of his life, the Hoka Hey Motorcycle Challenge, a 13,860-mile race through the lost highways and party towns and Indian reservations of the lower 48 states in pursuit of hundreds of thousands of dollars in prize money. I had come to the desert to watch, in a professional sort of way, on assignment for a national newsmagazine. My journalistic partner, the famous war photographer, was booked on the next redeye into Sky Harbor.

Sprawling in ambition, grandiose in scale and haphazard in execution, the Hoka Hey promised to harness the mythology of the

open road for a test of wills meant to publicize the plight of the Lakota. Money was not to be the true reward. "By becoming a Hoka Hey
Challenger," the promotional materials proclaimed, "your name will
be immortalized."

After relinquishing my license, Big Jim suggested sharing a
meal as prerequisite to a formal interview. This was his way. In the
brief time of our acquaintance, he was forever offering to share
things — his cigarettes, a hunk of chocolate chip muffin — always
in ceremonial fashion. I said okay to the dinner plan, and he laughed,
a guffawing sort of laugh that managed to ring both nervous and
dismissive at the same time. Admirers and detractors alike draw cre-
dence from his laugh. It sounds like "Whuh-huh-huh-ha."

* * *

Ours is a nation of highways, 160,000 miles by the count of the United
States Department of Transportation. They are connectors, yes, often
likened to blood vessels sustaining the far-flung organs of an increasingly urbanized society, but driving them is fast becoming one of the
last disconnected things you can do. In the canyons, in the Badlands,
in the Appalachians, the signal fades. You get no bars. You can't check
in. You can't become the electronic mayor of nowhere.

This has come to pass for hardship. Roll over, Jack Kerouac.
Peter Fonda, shut your eyes. In the three decades since Brock Yates led
the Cannonball Baker Sea-to-Shining Sea Memorial Trophy Dash in
celebration of a devil-may-care strain of American freedom, various
promoters of road racing have introduced corporate sponsorships,
reality television and the self-flagellating ethos of endurance sport.
The open road itself, undiminished as a symbol of possibility, now
spans a chastened and increasingly desperate land.

In my own travels, I have seen some unlikely elaborations on
the timeless appeal of the basic speed contest. I have seen turbine
powerboats make laps at 200 miles an hour in 6-foot seas off Key West.
I have seen cyclists cross the snow-laden and buckling crust of the
Little Susitna River north of Anchorage. I have seen men strap electronic heart monitors to their chests in preparation for the qualifying
rounds of a 260-mile canoe odyssey said to prompt hallucinations

in which airborne gunmen strafe the Guadalupe River. Once, in the Green Mountains of Vermont, I watched a British Royal Marine stumble off the Appalachian Trail to vanquish a local financier in a daylong test of stamina known as The Death Race.

The question is always: why? The answers never satisfy.

But those who promote long-distance contests of speed on the public roadways constitute a separate breed. Many view themselves as keepers of a flame, libertarians in the most strictly traditional sense, with one significant concession to conventional authority. For legal reasons, they tend to avoid invoking the word "race." While specifics vary from state to state, the Arizona transportation code defines racing as "the use of one or more vehicles in an attempt to outgain or outdistance another vehicle or prevent another vehicle from passing," classified on first offense as a misdemeanor punishable by a $250 fine and on subsequent offense as a felony punishable by 10 days in jail. Euphemisms such as "rally" and "challenge" provide some small degree of plausible deniability for the organizers of such events.

In the case of the Hoka Hey Motorcycle Challenge, any insistence on semantic accuracy (first to the finish line wins = race) seemed to pose a distinct liability. The inaugural running, held in the summer of 2010, had already left a trail of complaints documented in police reports, filed with state attorneys general, posted online and recounted in local newspapers. The wife of one participant, according to the *Rapid City Journal*, had attested, "My husband would have never chosen to support this event had he known, up front, what Jim Red Cloud's real agenda was."

This time around, Big Jim intended to control the narrative.

* * *

Inside Chester's Harley-Davidson, a sprawling expanse of impervious cover planted with permanent signage evoking a theme park version of the Old West, a new placard offered a warning.

"You Are Being Photographed," the sign said. "Please Be Advised that The Movement Inc. is filming in this area in connection with an entertainment production." Down a hallway, crew members had turned a windowless room into a sound stage for the kind of talking head segments known as confessionals. Covering the saloon murals on the walls, they set up a backdrop depicting the race logo, a skull in a headdress. They stacked expensive camera gear, professional-grade light fixtures and laptops galore in no discernible order. One by one, they brought in each rider, wired him for sound and quizzed him about his motivations. A typical answer went, "I just felt like I have to be here. This is where I'm supposed to be."

Big Jim's wife, Beth, sat at a desk near the back of the makeshift green room, managing logistics for the race. Despite weeks of conversations in advance of my arrival, she now deferred reflexively to the filmmakers. "Meet and greet with the challengers, unless I hear otherwise," she said, indicating the film producers as the controlling authority on matters of access to the race. "It's just a courtesy, working with them as closely as we intend to on the future of the Challenge."

Back East, the newsmagazine financing my travels seemed most interested in the spectacle of the race. Having seen my share of races, I had my eye on the elusive figure running the show, Big Jim. But either way, his personal storytelling apparatus seemed like a force to be reckoned with.

Take me to your leader, I told the nearest p.a. In the parking lot, I soon found the film producer, David Roma, a New York native in his mid-30s, dressed in a Panama hat and white sunglasses with outsize earphones clamped around his neck. He strolled the grounds with a gregarious yet permanently distracted air of authority, giving the impression that his business card, if he carried one, would have said "auteur." He had brought along his wife and young child, who spent much of their day playing in the race office.

After training as a classical pianist at the Juilliard School, Roma said, he had made his career in Hollywood. His credits ranged from "Gasland," an award-winning documentary on the drilling technique known as hydraulic fracturing, to "Snoop Dogg's Father Hood," a reality television series for which he'd served as executive producer of such episodes as "Who'z Tha Boss." As we talked, he casually disclosed that he had become a show runner by age 26, making $1 million a year by age 30. He smoked like it was a contest and dropped names like it was the tie-breaker. He mentioned Barry Diller and some other movie people I'd heard of, but he spoke with more passion when our talk turned to the race. Through his work on a program called "Biker Build-Off," he explained, he had acquired some familiarity with motorcycle culture and some renown within same, leading to his recruitment by Big Jim.

"Jim adopted me and hoka-heyed me, which I'd only seen in the movies," Roma said. Before I could elicit a description of that particular rite, he went on, "There's a ceremony in a couple days where I get an eagle feather, and that ties me to them in this life and the next. They're an incredibly spiritual group, the Sioux."

His film, he said, would harness the entertainment value of the motorcycle race to raise money for the tribe, thus belatedly fulfilling certain promises made the prior year by Big Jim. In practical terms, Roma planned to deploy three camera teams: one to track the front of the pack, a second to trail behind and a third posted at each subsequent checkpoint for relief. Also, he said, "Parts I'm going to be filming by helicopter."

While his budget piqued my journalistic curiosity, his armada raised more immediate practical considerations. The newsmagazine had provided expense accounts for the famous war photographer and me, but money was tight. Drawing on a $2,000 line of credit I had taken out to pay my way while awaiting reimbursement, I'd already spent $234 on a one-way ticket to Phoenix, rented a car on an open-ended contract and charmed my way through some cash-flow-related indignity at the hotel check-in, with no way of knowing when or from where I would fly home to the address so ostentatiously memorialized by Big Jim. In any event, no line item on the magazine's accounting department forms seemed to cover high-performance private aircraft. As professional storytellers, I mean to say, the famous war photographer and I were finding ourselves outgunned.

For the moment, my questions about the film's financing would have to wait. At the pace of his undiscarded Manhattan accent, Roma expounded on the legacy of broken treaties, citing numbers of slain Indians. Thirty-five million was the figure he gave. The race, he said, "was created as a vision quest. Jim and his grandfather, in a

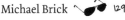

sweat, had a vision of this. They brought people together from every race, color and creed to ride."

He went on: "The voice of the Indians is a whisper right now. We barely hear it. The idea of bringing all these men together is trying to turn that whisper into a roar. Sort of like the roar of a Harley engine. They thought they were signing up for a half-million-dollar endurance contest. But really they were sent on a vision quest."

"There's a lot of variables in a story like this," Roma said. "But I can control it by setting three fundamental themes."

He had already chosen: Transformation, accountability and spirituality. As we wrapped up the conversation, he made one more disclosure. Before the ride was done, he said, death might come to the owner of the Harley dealership, E.B. Chester, who was 67. It had been foretold, he said, by Big Jim.

* * *

The riders favored Street Glides and Road Kings, the big touring models equipped with wide seats, full fairings and rubber-mounted drivetrains built to cradle the buttocks for the long haul. They arrived aboard black bikes, blue bikes, black and blue bikes, orange bikes, white bikes, brown bikes and red bikes, limited by the rules of the race to Harley-Davidson models equipped with 6.2-liter maximum-capacity V-Twin engines. They displayed the names of regional dealerships and of energy drink makers. They flew the flags of the United States of America and its prisoners of war. They showed proof of insurance, submitted to odometer photographs and accepted $60 electronic devices designed to relay time-stamp signals from the inner windscreen just below the triple-tree fork to a satellite capable of monitoring speed and position at the precision of a parking space. They signed entry forms pledging to obey all applicable laws of the road, plus waivers for the film production company. They studied a rough outline of the course, which traversed the country twice southerly and three times northerly.

Against a 16-day deadline, the riders would trace both coasts and much of the Gulf. They would not learn the exact route until it was handed out piecemeal at each of more than a dozen checkpoints.

They would take the long way around Lake Michigan. They would pass the Hoover Dam, Death Valley, the Golden Gate Bridge, the Bitterroot Range, Wind River Canyon, the Mississippi River, the Blue Ridge Mountains and the Natchez Trace Parkway. They would pass Mount Rushmore, Half Dome and Bourbon Street. They would take 318 curves in 11 miles through the Tail of the Dragon speedway at Deal's Gap, North Carolina. They would press on through the Pennsylvania boondocks. The finish line stood across the border, in Sydney, Nova Scotia.

The conditions, including a $1,000 entry fee and a significant time commitment, favored so-called RUBs, or Rich Urban Bikers. The turnout represented a diverse spectrum of humanity by the standards of motorcycle culture, which remains at least as racially segregated as general culture (the National Bikers Roundup, held the same weekend, drew thousands of black riders; the Hoka Hey drew approximately none).

The riders gathered in the convection afternoon, a truck driver, a software developer, a lesbian couple, several diabetics and a good deal more military veterans. Members of the film crew wandered around, gauging the potential of each rider's personal history as a story pitch. A guy who had lost his mobile home was racing for money; a breast cancer survivor was racing for what's known as awareness; a guy whose oxygen tank had failed during the previous year's race was dragging two oxygen tanks.

"A lot of swan songs," a production assistant named Marcus was saying. "There's a lot who want to go out on their own terms. I'm getting a sense of lost Americans."

There were riders like Charles R. Laws, known as Ranger, a retired First Sergeant of A Company, Third Battalion, who wore an eye patch and a wispy beard, inspecting his 2011 Road King. He'd decorated the machine, a 62nd birthday gift from his wife, with a bumper sticker that said "I ♥ Hooters" and another that said "Vietnam — I Served." As he told it, "I was bailing hay one day, state of Delaware, and a guy come by in a pickup. He said, 'Hoka hey.' He said, 'It's a great run we're putting together.' I called that day and talked to Beth." His memories of the inaugural run, if somewhat imprecise, seemed fond.

"The further we rode, the harder it got; the harder it got, the better it got," Laws said. As far as his ranking among the finishers was concerned, "they never told me and I didn't want to ask." This year, he said, "I figure I've got as good a chance as anybody else. It'll be as hard on them as it is on me."

There were riders like Terry Meyer, aka Terry Rogue, 45, identifiable by the word "Rogue" tattooed in cursive across his Mohawked scalp. He had been racing bikes since childhood, he said, following the circuit from Motocross to Supermoto to Enduro, in which he once injured his neck sliding off a cliff. His story, as unverifiable in parts as his official name, included the loss of both parents to a single motorcycle accident in 2003. Undeterred by all the motorcycle-related carnage visited upon his life, he had ridden the inaugural Hoka Hey in 2010 aboard a Bare-Knuckle Chopper, a bike with no suspension, custom-made by a company in Hawk Point, Missouri (motto: "You Want Cheap & Foreign Go Someplace Else"). "Since my parents were killed, it's been really hard," he said. "I just started finding out what spiritual is. I felt it. I experienced it last year. I rode with my mom and dad. They were there with me. I felt it for the last third of the ride." His new training regimen included an 800-calorie diet, on which he had lost 39 pounds. Though recent injuries had him in a neck brace, he was out to win. "The strategy is not to race other people," he said. "It's within myself. Get up front, run up front. I'm not trying to come off as cocky, but we're here to do a job."

Then there was Whittany Crum, 23, who had secured the use of a 2011 Street Glide from sponsors at a dealership in the Carolinas. In her estimation, the heft of the machine, with a wide saddle and highway pegs designed to stretch the legs, would weigh against her relative inexperience to carry her across the finish line. She'd served as Miss Hoka Hey the prior year, recruited by Big Jim, whom she described as a former distant relative. To prepare, she had tried weightlifting, but quit the exercise routine in favor of more riding time. For the transcontinental excursion, she had packed a pair of jeans, a couple T-shirts, a hygiene kit, rain gear and a leather bedroll, plus the music of Pink Floyd and Avenged Sevenfold, which she planned to play at maximum volume to overcome the highway noise. Her strategy, she said, was to sleep four hours a night, stay hydrated, snack on the bike, "just keep going and try not to miss a turn."

And then there was Elijah Whirlwind Horse, 24, who identified himself as a grandson of Oliver Red Cloud, the Lakota chief who has held a position of authority on the Pine Ridge Reservation well into his 90s. Whirlwind Horse, who hangs drywall for a living, learned to ride on dirt bikes, acquired a 2009 FLHX Street Glide as a loaner for the race and trained principally by sunbathing to inure himself to the elements, which had proven an insurmountable obstacle in the inaugural race. "Rained, snowed, boiled, everything," he recalled. "But other than that it was a good run." His Crazy Horse Harley had locked up somewhere in Arkansas, prompting a rescue by his uncle, but he was back for the second running with a sense of elevated stakes. Displaying a fresh warrior tattoo, he likened his role in the race to riding in front of a hunting expedition, or into battle.

"With that camera," he told me, "we're going to get a lot of voices to hear the cry of the people who don't have water."

All the while, working the perimeter — I don't want to say lurking — was Big Jim, chatting up the bikers, smoking those Reds, laughing that laugh, "Whuh-huh-huh-ha."

* * *

Big Jim: By the account of his wife, Beth, who is eight years his junior, James Durham followed military service in Vietnam with a stint teaching a class on cultural resources at a small college in Ohio. There they met. She was expecting to make dream-catchers. Instead, she received private lessons in scrimshaw, the delicate art of engraving bone. "'Intense' was the first thought," she said. "'Brooding' is another word that comes to mind. I didn't come to know the passion behind the man until later."

As Beth told it, the couple moved around the country through much of the 1990s, while she was serving in the Navy. Eventually they ended up in South Dakota, on the outskirts of the Pine Ridge Reservation, where he pursued an artistic career. She did not want to say more.

Later, through an exceedingly popular online merchant, I acquired for the sum of $12.27 a mint condition copy of "Sacred Buffalo:

The Lakota Way for a New Beginning," a memoir published in 1996 under the name James G. Durham. In an author photo given prominent display on the dedications page, Big Jim wears a cowboy hat, a massive oval belt buckle, a Western shirt open to the third button and a ponytail draped over his heart. He stares into the camera, partly obscuring his book's ostensible subject, a full bovine skeleton scrimshawed with ornate imagery depicting a Sundance, a Hanbleceya, a Yuwipi and other Lakota ceremonies. In a 186-page account written with a co-author, he describes seven years of work on the sculpture, a project meant to foster racial harmony, world peace and a renewed connection with the Creator. He likens his work to "waltzing with God."

"I dreamed as a child that I was walking on a big wall and talking to millions of people," he writes. "Maybe that dream is coming true now."

Court records tell the rest of the story. The Sacred Buffalo toured the country until it was damaged by a chair thrown from the viewing gallery at a museum in St. Johnsbury, Vermont. Big Jim sued the vandals, valuing his artistry and 17,000 hours of labor at $1.2 million. After one of the defendants filed a handwritten response accusing him of collusion in an insurance fraud scheme, Big Jim dropped his lawsuit. Litigation against his investors ended in similar stalemate. The insurance claim was paid. The vandals served jail time. Big Jim faced no criminal charges. To others similarly situated, the experience might have conveyed a lesson in humility. Not Big Jim.

"You're weak," he said when I finally cornered him in the hallway. "You're like that child over there. You may come out of this with more than you bargained for. You may be willing to hang from a tree by your chest for others."

After some airing of grievances concerning various practitioners of journalism, his tone shifted from gruff to cryptic. I asked about his background, particularly how he had come to acquire the name he was using in promotional materials, Jim Red Cloud. He said he had renounced the surname of a stepfather "who broke most of my bones with shovels."

Though he glossed over the part about getting to know the Lakota, his book was helpful on that score as well. In an early chapter, he tells of meeting a man who carried an eagle feather on a visit to the Vietnam Wall. The chance encounter led to a cross-country drive on his motorcycle to attend a Sundance held for war veterans in Green Grass, South Dakota. During the ride, he writes, he encountered a hundred miles of sleet, bled from his face and screamed at the Creator. Upon arrival, he ate some soup, sat in a sweat lodge and performed the dance. He came away convinced that his efforts would help bring home prisoners of war.

In an adoption ceremony called a hunka, Big Jim told me, he took his new last name from the descendants of Makhpiya-Luta, Scarlet Cloud, the 19th-century warrior who had dealings with the Pawnee, Crow, Ute and Shoshone tribes. The ceremony, he said, is "one of the seven rites of the Sioux nation. It's looked at like God made a mistake. And when you choose your relatives, it's always stronger, because it's chosen." He said his name change had been made official "in a court of law." He did not specify state, federal or tribal. When I asked about the records, he said the name change had been sealed, which is possible for victims of domestic violence. He promised to tell me the rest later. Then he walked off. Ten minutes later, he came back.

"I was just thinking about you," he said. "You're a lucky guy. You must have done something right to get put in the middle of this."

* * *

The conditions on the Pine Ridge Reservation are a documented national disgrace, well beyond any dispute. A recent EPA report, citing a study by South Dakota State University, estimated that a third of its homes lack basic filtration, sewage and electricity. In the 2010 Census, Shannon County reported the lowest per capita income in the country, with unemployment estimated around 70 percent.

But Big Jim's memory of his own effort to rectify the situation more or less matches the complaints posted online. Vowing to bring clean running water to the reservation, he named his motorcycle race after an exclamation (which loosely translates as "Let's go!") attributed to Crazy Horse. He openly portrayed the inaugural event as a fundraising trick perpetrated in his greater wisdom for the good of the Lakota. "I said, 'Well, actually, I lied to you,'" he told me, recounting his speech to riders assembled in Key West, Florida, for the 2010 race. "'I didn't tell you the whole reason we're here. We're here to get water. I had to bring you here to do it.'"

His detractors say he failed to deliver on his promises, which included a winner-take-all prize of $500,000 in gold and payments to several charities. Along the circuitous 8,300-mile course from Key West to Homer, Alaska, two of the riders perished: Charles C. Lynn in Wyoming and Kenneth J. Greene in Alaska. Several more also crashed, including Vik Livingston of Seattle, who hit a pair of bicyclists. Attorneys general of Florida and South Dakota logged formal complaints. Among other internal controversies, a lasting grudge developed between two riders who crossed the finish line simultaneously, Frank Kelly of South Carolina and Will Barclay of Florida. Determining a winner, Big Jim said in an open letter to his critics, involved polygraph testing. After disqualifying Kelly for skipping a so-called phantom checkpoint at the home of his adopted namesake in Pine Ridge, Big Jim paid Barclay not in gold but in wire-transferred cash, which seems to have sufficed.

The charities got nothing. In the intervening year, during which he lost his adult son to pneumonia, Big Jim envisioned a new course to intersect the old, a medicine wheel drawn across the continent. He cast the second running, longer by half again, as a test of the warrior spirit, meant to "foster a greater appreciation for the earth, its people and the connections that create harmony and love."

* * *

Dressed out in denim and leather, the riders exchanged bear hugs, re-introduced their wives and told one another things like, "Can't resist another run, huh?" A crowd soon formed around Will Barclay, 51, winner of the 2010 inaugural race. He was wearing short pants, a straw hat concealing an ice pack and an Evel Knievel T-shirt displaying a big red, white and blue 1. His regimen was the stuff of legend: A veteran of triathlons, he trained in the Himalayas, slept an hour a day and fitted himself with a catheter aboard an Electra Glide he called Excalibur.

"I raised the bar last year," Barclay said. "This year everybody knows what I did, and they're doing it."

Barclay's dominance as a participant paled beside his role as a fixer. After receiving his prize money in 2010, he had worked contacts from his day job as a Gulfstream pilot to build legitimacy for the race, which in modern terms means not just money but also cameras. His sometime employer, Hamish Harding, a British financier who wears multiple belt accessories and calls his holding company the Action Group, was providing the money, about $1 million by his own estimation, which seemed to account for the financing of Hollywood Dave Roma & Co.

To sweeten the pot, E.B. Chester had secured a sponsorship from Harley-Davidson Motor Company, which agreed to award the winner a new motorcycle (of retail value between $29,599 and $36,499) in addition to the quarter-million dollar cash prize promised by Big Jim. Prophecy of his demise notwithstanding, Old Man Chester looked all right to me health-wise, though of course anything could happen on the road. He said he'd acquired his first Harley in 1958, operated dealerships across the country and ridden in the inaugural race. "It was a different experience than some people expected," he said with diplomatic understatement. "But it was about like-minded individuals coming together and doing the almost impossible." To help expand the ambitions of the race, he said, he had personally designed the circuitous new course. He was also planning to host the sendoff party. Selling the Harley people on the sponsorship had been no small task. "I tried to convince them that all the carping last year was from people who didn't finish and were carping about it because they couldn't do it," he said. "Two people died last year, but if you count out the miles and calculate the deaths per mile, there were fewer deaths in this than there were riding in the street."

His argument seemed to have carried the day. Some men from Harley-Davidson Inc., including Keith E. Wandell, the chief executive, were making their way to the dealership for the opening ceremony, where they would stand onstage alongside Big Jim.

* * *

Inside the office on the eve of the race, workers sold T-shirts, hoodies and a $200 set of race logo patches to the riders. Beth worked the phones. Her husband had gone to the airport, she said, to pick up "the holy man."

Late in the afternoon, Big Jim arrived with Steve Dubray, 52, a former schoolteacher who serves as a tribal elder on the reservation. In a salt and pepper ponytail, Dubray projected a manner of deep relaxation. When I took him aside to ask about the ceremony in which the tribe had adopted Big Jim, he gave confirmation. He defined the word hunka—poetically, I thought—as meaning "more than our own blood."

"My people are resilient," Dubray said. "Very strong, unwilling to bow down. So much so that they have such a hard life. And still, we're rich. We're rich in spirituality. It's the only thing that keeps us together as a nation. We have one of the poorest counties in South Dakota. And again, we're rich. We have family. We have extended family, and we have prayer, which a lot of people don't have. And we have connection to the land. The sacred Black Hills."

As for Big Jim's race, he said, "with the riders carrying the message for us, the event carrying the message for us, we hope people will say, 'Remember that ride they had? Well, they were riding for the Lakota people.'"

Outside under the long summer sunset, more riders arrived to await the final gathering, which was billed as part sendoff party, part pre-race briefing and part invocation. The famous war photographer, who had a habit of uncorking some pretty disturbing anecdotes on little to no provocation, seemed to be making friends easily in this crowd. He shot portraits of the bikers. He made a good effort to coax Big Jim in front of the camera.

For the famous war photographer and me, there remained the matter of logistics. When I broached the subject of transportation with David Roma, he quizzed me at length about my intentions, asking whether my account would slander the poor Lakota. It would not, I said. To the contrary, I told him, I was hoping to meet the patriarch of the Red Cloud lineage in order to get a handle on Big Jim.

At that, I secured passage for myself aboard the film production vehicles. But I soon witnessed the limits of Roma's ability to stage-manage the presentation of the race. A few hours before the opening ceremony, he introduced his crew to a new contestant, whom he described as a former sitcom writer. I did not catch this man's name. I did hear him talk of plans to chronicle his experience in a motorcycle memoir. Roma seemed enthusiastic. His cameramen started setting up an interview. But less than an hour later, I watched Big Jim stomp across the room toward his wife.

"What are we going to get?" Big Jim asked Beth. "Put a number on it."

"He said he's doing a book, and he's going to give a portion to the charities," she said.

"A penny: Here's your portion," Big Jim bellowed. "What does that mean?"

An hour after that, out in the parking lot, I watched the sitcom writer shake Big Jim's hand and say he was sorry things had turned out the way they did and drive off into the desert. For reasons I did not care to probe, no such financial demands had been made in exchange for my own access to the race, but Big Jim turned to me with an explanation anyway: "You earned the right to talk to me, because you ate food with me," he said. "When you leave Pine Ridge, you'll understand all this. Whuh-huh-huh-ha."

He meant the chocolate chip muffin. Our dinner never happened.

* * *

Before nightfall, the riders assembled in a sweltering garage where the energy drinks were free, the fans were useless and the sound system was blaring Bob Seger & the Silver Bullet Band. The ceremony was about to begin. At its climax, we were told, we would have the rare opportunity to witness a captive bald eagle soaring in flight to symbolize the spirit of the race.

"I hope to God you're ready," Big Jim intoned. He pounded out a rhythm on the microphone. As the riders joined up the beat, clapping hands, banging bottles and slapping chairs, he told us about the superiority of Harley-Davidson among motorcycle brands. He laughed into the microphone. He called the riders "the purest of all warriors."

Then a guitarist sang happy birthday to Beth. That was nice.

Big Jim introduced the holy man as his brother. Steve Dubray said a prayer in Lakota. He thanked the riders "for being our voice."

Big Jim said he was going to say one more thing. Then he said several more things. He said he expected his critics to butcher him on the Internet. He talked about the price of humanity. He talked about the demise of the Indians. He told the riders, "You are our last voice. It's almost over."

He said he was about to cry. Then he laughed, "Whuh-huh-huh-ha."

The gathering was not done. Not by a long shot. It was very, very, very hot in the garage. In her tactical briefing, Beth asked the riders to help their competitors in the event of a breakdown. She called them brothers and sisters. She told them to obey the law. "It's you against the highway," she said. "It's not a race." She passed the microphone to a Harley executive, who said, "It's the spirit of adventure that's the heart and soul of this nation. We salute you."

Then this happened: A trainer from a bird rescue group arrived onstage with a 4-year-old eagle named Sonora perched on his glove. A hundred cell phone cameras rose to document the moment. Steve Dubray and his granddaughter sang a song in Lakota, translated as, "Grandfather, thank you, I pray from this circle of life, thank you, thank you grandfather."

"Sonora, hup," called the trainer. Sonora, attached at the talons to a rope, shedding a great flurry of feathers, flew in a line-drive path straight from the stage to another trainer positioned on the floor. Then the doors opened, the light came streaming in, a wave of fresh dry heat replaced the stale dry heat of the garage and the riders yelled, "Hoka hey!"

PaRt Two

The Carefree Highway
August 5, 2011

In the windless blueblack of a Friday morning, the riders lined up six abreast, smoking and tinkering and cursing and studying maps and posing for flash photos. An hour before dawn, the organizers handed out cards specifying a turn-by-turn route to the first checkpoint, a Harley dealership in Las Vegas. Any divergence, they said, would result in disqualification. Pocket flashlights emerged. From high above in the darkened sky, a satellite sent signals to the tracking devices attached to the bikes, which sent the signals on to the nearest cellular tower, which sent the signals on to laptop computer screens monitored by the organizers and filmmakers.

The holy man held his granddaughter aloft. Together they sang a lament in their ancestral tongue. The riders gathered, looking solemn. The holy man gave a blessing. At 5:38 a.m., Dave Roma's helicopter moved into position overhead. Five minutes later, Big Jim crushed out a cigarette.

"Mount up!" he called. A hundred engines revved. Beth boarded a yellow pace bike to lead the riders out of town. The holy man raised a torch, christening the ride in smoke. And they were off.

* * *

There's a scene in the movie "Back to the Future" where Marty McFly, played by Michael J. Fox, arrives at the home of his mother's family in 1955. Watching his Uncle Joey, who will become a prison inmate as an adult, squirm around in a playpen, he says, "So you're my Uncle Joey. Better get used to these bars, kid."

The Internet Movie Database does not list a credit for the actor who portrayed the Baby Uncle Joey in that scene, so there is no easy way to verify the claim made by Leonard Williams, 28, the driver of the camera crew van I flagged down as the race began. I figured he was telling the truth; otherwise, what an imaginative thing to make up. At any rate, he talked the talk of a streetwise film industry Angeleno, with organizational skills suggesting that some other advantage had factored into his selection for the job of film crew van driver. By his own admission, he had slept only 45 minutes overnight. Accompanied by two even younger cameramen and their cooler of vegan snacks, Williams trailed the riders down Country Club Drive. As the race neared the outskirts of town, a neat column of bikes split into small groups, partnerships and solo riders. It soon became apparent that other than me, none of the guys in the van had picked up a route card. They debated turning back. My internal monologue weighed journalistic qualms about affecting the situation against the journalistic imperative to make it to the Pine Ridge Reservation, where I hoped to gauge the true nature of Big Jim. I handed over the route card, which prescribed an exact path to the checkpoint in 30 turns following this format:

Turn	On To	Ride	To Mile
L	Shea Blvd W Into Fountain Hills	2.3	18.0

The sky glowed orange. "Yo, man, we got a man down already," Williams said, but it turned out one of the riders had merely stopped to take pictures. At 6 a.m., barely a quarter of an hour into the race, we spotted Big Jim and his entourage, in no apparent rush, fueling up at a gas station.

"It's a beautiful day to be alive," observed a rider wearing a patch that said "White Boy." "You know how Jim said he's trying to do such a great thing? He already has."

Williams steered the van toward the Carefree Highway, through a landscape of scrub, cactus and power lines. The sun announced itself over the distant hills of the Tonto National Forest. To pass the time, I opened the film production "bible," which gave detailed story guides and camera angle instructions.

"The epic scale of the challenge, taking these men from all walks of life and having them cover 14,000 miles from Arizona to Nova Scotia for the largest sum of money for any motorcycle challenge, makes it an interesting challenge to film," Roma had written. "However, the true story lies not in the race, but mostly on the reservation it was conceived."

When I looked up, the riders were nowhere in sight. Williams professed not to mind, though he spent the next several miles twirling an unlit Marlboro Light between his fingers in a way that appeared to resemble minding. We passed through Carefree, where the citizens were up power-walking past the yoga studios of a faux frontier town with streets called Bloody Basin Road and Tranquil Trail. From the back seat of the van, one of the vegan cameramen announced that Big Jim, according to the tracking devices, was still back in Mesa.

"One example of transformation is when a rider has gone through a loss or divorce and takes on this challenge to help overcome their loss," I read in the film production bible. "For the riders who are not professional endurance riders, taking on the challenge of riding 14,000 miles where winning could require perhaps 20 hours sleep over 13 days, there has to be something motivating them."

Climbing into the Bradshaw Mountains, Williams spotted some Harleys at the Ranch House Restaurant. The vegan cameramen ran around the parking lot like it was a firefight until a waitress came out and yelled, "Hey, come in here and take pictures! Gotta get some business somehow."

I went to sit with E.B. Chester, the 67-year-old owner of the dealership back in Mesa, who was riding the race with no evident designs on victory. He is a wealthy man already.

"Since we set here, half the field has gone by," Chester said. He had cleaned his plate. "Nothing's going to happen today. They're running on adrenaline."

The first part was wrong, the second prophetic. Not far from Yarnell Hill, a steep granite outcrop winding under juniper trees fit for Dr. Seuss, the film crew came across what appeared to be a downed helicopter surrounded by ambulances. Williams parked the van.

"Hey guys," he said, rushing up to a rescue worker. "I don't mean to pry, but a friend of mine, David Roma, is flying around in a helicopter out here. I just want to make sure that's not David Roma."

It was not, he was told.

In fact, the helicopter belonged to the medics. The man on the stretcher was rider No. 186, Gregory Shafer, who had lost control of his bike on a turn through an upward incline. Another rider, Bill Aviles, 50, a retired fire captain from Marietta, California, had gotten to him first. "The sun was pulling up at kind of a weird angle, and all I could see was the dust," Aviles later told me. "It was a hairpin turn, and I knew somebody was going off the road." Finding Shafer face down in the bushes, 50 feet below the road and 15 above his bike, Aviles had tested him for stimulus response, removed his helmet and cleared his airway. Somebody had called the authorities. Medical transport had been arranged.

Moving on toward Prescott, we came across Big Jim and company at a filling station. He did not offer an explanation for his sudden progress, though our long stops at the diner and the rescue scene may have played a role. I asked whether he'd heard about the crash.

"Greg Shafer, yeah," Big Jim said. "He went down. He ain't dead though. Pretty ugly. It's just a dangerous game we play. Everybody knows it."

I was waiting for that laugh, but it never came.

* * *

Crossing the Verde Valley, where the landscape turns to pebbles and mesquite, red, gold and green, the vegan cameramen worried over their handheld GoPros. The van crossed through small towns built into mountainsides, over high elevation passages where tarpaulins held back looming boulders and around curves better suited to the bikers ahead in the distance. A laptop computer in the backseat showed the riders in three main packs. Williams found a shortcut, parked the van near the next filling station and executed the film industry equivalent of a stakeout.

"Dude," said Travis, the older of the vegan cameramen, approaching a rider on a baby blue Ultra Classic. His interview opened with a question about the crash scene.

"Is he all right?" Travis asked.

"I don't know," the rider said. "His bike wasn't."

The interview did not last long. Other riders came and went, attending to fluids, checking maps and applying sunscreen.

"They didn't want to talk about it, but I could tell it was very heavy on them," said Alex, the younger vegan cameraman, once we got back in the van. Talk turned to the leaders of the race, Frank Kelly and the reigning champ, Will Barclay. Somebody said they were running neck and neck. We missed the next exit. Determined not to fall behind again, Williams swerved the van onto the entrance ramp, heading up a blind hill against traffic.

"This is some hoka hey, man, good day to die," he mumbled, gunning the motor. Fifty miles an hour. Sixty. The vegan cameramen fell silent. Sixty-five miles an hour. Zero visibility up the entrance ramp. Seventy-five miles an hour. Time stood still. I found a grip on the door handle. Good day or no, I did not intend to leave this mortal coil in a rented van with Baby Uncle Joey and his vegan cameramen.

At the top of the ramp, Williams swerved back onto the service road. "Man, sometimes you just got to keep going," he said.

"Hoka hey," said Travis.

Williams said, "Hoka hey."

* * *

Hollywood Dave Roma had no trouble beating the rest of us to the first checkpoint in Las Vegas, traveling by means of an SJ-30 long-range light business jet with leather bucket seats, golden cup holders and a cruising speed of Mach 0.83, a conveyance his benefactor described as "kind of like a Ferrari-in-the-sky type of deal."

Over the weekend, the remaining riders reached the city. I wish I could report some gripping stuff on this score, but aside from the events I've mentioned, the actual racing mostly involved majestic scenery punctuated by reluctant stops for gas and sunscreen application. The remaining contestants devoted numbingly long passages in the saddle to the task of remaining awake, upright and alive. Perhaps Roma will handle his version of these events via montage. The reader's able mind will suffice for my purposes, though I can offer two bits of color recorded in my notes under the influence of my own sleep-deprivation:

Near the Hoover Dam, a billboard promotes a range where you can shoot a fully automatic machine gun, if you are unable to otherwise keep yourself entertained in Las Vegas.

Closer into the city, another billboard advertising the Grand Canyon Skywalk depicts an Indian in full headdress pointing the way to said skywalk.

Roll montage: Following new route cards, the riders lit out from Vegas to checkpoints in Reno, Nevada; Great Falls, Montana; Idaho Falls, Idaho; and on toward the great biker haven of Sturgis, South Dakota. While the filmmakers set up a command center at a hotel on the Strip, I spent the next four days at the Orleans, a discount casino where I financed the rest of my reporting trip with a few successful sessions at the craps tables. The famous war photographer bailed. By Tuesday morning, the satellite tracking devices showed the winners of the previous year's race, Will Barclay and Frank Kelly, back in the lead again, heading south out of the Broken Spoke campground along the Black Hills National Forest toward the "phantom checkpoint" at Pine Ridge.

Part Three

The Pine Ridge Reservation, South Dakota
August 9, 2011

At a private airport near the Vegas Strip, Hamish Harding made arrangements to lift off in his SJ-30. I settled into the cabin, scanning his business card, which listed separate mobile phone numbers in Dubai, Saudi Arabia, the United Kingdom, the United States and India. Harding assured me his plane was pressurized to replicate sea level conditions up to an elevation of 41,000 feet, which he said was better than the Concorde or the space shuttle. That sounded fine to me. It certainly qualified as an upgrade from the van.

Dave Roma took the seat beside me, juggling two cellphones. On the first, he appeared to be putting off a creditor. On the second, he directed his camera crews into position. Then he opened his laptop to review some research on the life expectancy of the Lakota. "This is not something you force-feed Americans," he said. "It's not really about pointing fingers. But masked as entertainment, it's like giving someone medicine with peanut butter on it."

The SJ-30 made short work of the Wasatch Mountains. At a stopover in Grand Junction, Colorado, Harding fumbled in his pockets for the $50 landing fee. He was only carrying hundreds. Roma settled the bill. The jet flew high over lush farmland to the airport at Rapid City, South Dakota, where a Harley promoter named Ed LeClere was waiting in a black Ford King Ranch F350 Super Duty Lariat pickup with the speakers playing R.E.O. Speedwagon at top volume. On the road to the reservation, LeClere provided an update on the race.

"We've been watching the speed, and Beth's going to talk to them, because 120 miles an hour is not cool," LeClere said.

"That is absolutely not true," Harding countered, citing his own online observations of the motorcycle tracking devices. "Eighty-three is the highest I've seen so far, and most of the time they're at 70, 71. People are getting jealous and saying things that are not accurate."

Past the turnoff for Mount Rushmore, through a raw landscape broken by RV parks and mining companies, LeClere told Roma how efforts to secure additional race sponsors might be advanced by a "sizzle reel," and Roma said no problem.

"I mean, yeah, we're doing this to bring water to people on the reservation, but nobody knows that," LeClere said.

"That," said Roma, "is something my film will definitely change."

Sixty miles outside the reservation, LeClere pulled into a driveway to pick up a sleeping bag for Beth Durham. What a strange turn of events: Here we were, six days after my license inspection, at the home of Big Jim. He had a tipi in the yard, medicinal herbs hung out to dry on the porch and a drawing of a smiling nun holding a sharpened crucifix over a four-legged creature in the garage. I listened for the sound of laughter on the wind but soon grew distracted watching Roma demonstrate Big Jim's blowgun.

* * *

South of the Badlands, far from the highways, deep into the reservation, gravel roads run past outhouses, pools of standing green water, yards full of rusting automotive hulks, a roof where a dozen old tires have been littered or perhaps hoarded, shotgun shacks left to rot and rotted shacks not yet left. The speed limit drops to 45. Over a hill, Chief Oliver Red Cloud sat in a wheelchair on his wooden porch.

"How!" he called when we pulled up in the Ford. "Oh, boy."

The chief, a great-great-grandson of the legendary warrior, had a full head of white hair, a silver belt buckle in his jeans, a hearing aid in his ear and a Band-Aid on his hand, which felt all but hollow in my loosest grip. We made offerings of thanksgiving for safe passage on the reservation. Harding, on behalf of the film crew, presented a fistful of hundred-dollar bills. Separately, I presented an ounce of pipe tobacco, acquired for $3.78 back at the Grand Canal Shoppes Mall in the Venetian.

"I, myself, I'm the chief," Red Cloud told us. "I take care of the treaties. I have to know all the laws. United Nations, the Constitution, state laws. I have to think twice before I talk to my people. I have a big job. I'm 93 years old, and still going strong. New York, California, Washington, you name it, I'm there."

Harding said he wanted to see "the real Pine Ridge." When the chief had finished telling about it, I asked his opinion of Big Jim.

"Jim, he's a young man," the chief said. "And I had an older boy. And he went to law school in Rapid City. And somehow they meet each other in the Black Hills, bike riders. So my boy adopted him into Red Cloud family."

He pointed to the grave of his son Verdell, the oldest of six brothers. When he spoke again, his endorsement spread from Big Jim to the entire film crew: "He's in the Red Cloud family now. He comes all the time. He helps me all the time. And these boys work with him. I know them. They're good boys. They don't use alcohol, nothing."

The chief cast his gaze to the horizon. Somebody with a laptop said Will Barclay was leading the pack, with Frank Kelly 40 minutes behind. Up the hill to the left of the house, I paid my respects at the grave of Verdell Red Cloud. Down the hill to the right, I found some men preparing for a sweat in a lodge made of blankets, a tent, a hole in the ground and a woodpile for heating rocks. Horses whinnied in the hills. An eagle soared overhead. I asked about Big Jim.

"Jim's not just helping my grandpa," said Charles Red Cloud. "My grandpa's helping him. He's saying: 'Here's my adopted grand- son, and he's going to tell you that you're not living up to the treaties that you made.' You've got individuals on the Internet who say it's just about publicity, and it might be. I'm not directly involved. But I see he does what he tells my grandpa he's going to do. That's just my per- spective. Other people have their own."

When I asked about Big Jim's past, Charles said: "I don't know too much about Jim. I know he's been in the military. I know when he was younger he used to not be so ethical. But he changed his ways."

Then Warren Red Cloud spoke up: "I can put something in on Jim. You can tell a lot about a man by the way people talk about him when he's not there. And I've only heard good things about Jim."

"My grandfather, he's a very wise man," Charles said. "And he can read people. And he must see a lot of good in Jim, to support him in his cause. When he comes, it's always with a good heart."

"A man's words mean nothing," Warren said. "You know? It's his deeds that mean something. And Jim speaks with what he does."

Back up at the house, a baby was crying. Young men stood around smoking. A dog called Casino slept in the dirt. Sloppy Joes warmed on the stove. Riders would be passing through for the next week, bound for Grand Junction, Colorado; Santa Fe, New Mexico; Kansas City, Missouri; Oconomowoc, Wisconsin; Columbus, Ohio; Murfreesboro, Tennessee; Rocky Mount, North Carolina; Laconia, New Hampshire, and on into Nova Scotia.

In the kitchen, Chief Red Cloud sat in his wheelchair, quizzing the wife of Big Jim.

"I'm waiting," the chief said. "I'm not against you. I'm not against Jim Red Cloud, but he's got to make good. Because people got eyes and ears. They start using my picture and stuff, and people might say boo."

"There wouldn't be anything coming from Hoka Hey that you don't have the final word on," Beth told him. She went on: "Hoka Hey represents what we want for the Lakota people, that they can set out a goal and accomplish it. We're working hard toward something, Grandpa, and it's going to be slow."

The chief said: "That's a good dream. But we have to show something. They need water over here. If he did one thing, I could show the Lakota people, he's doing something."

The chief spoke at length of broken promises. He said: "So I have to watch that. Don't get me wrong. I'm not against you or nothing. But I'm involved in that. Because you have my name. But when people say booey, I have to be able to show them something."

"We know it's still got a lot of work to do," Beth said. "And we welcome your support."

"But I've got to see something beyond talk about it," the chief said. "I can't just support it. At least do one something."

"It's a lot of work to make people see things."

"And people are bad. You make one mistake, it gets you. When he comes back, we'll sit down and talk. At least he can start. Maybe put in one pipe."

From the front porch came a commotion. A rider was approaching. Big Jim, or maybe not. Rain clouds gathered in the twilight. The chief rolled out to see for himself.

Epilogue

February 2013

I'd seen enough. After a night's rest at the Prairie Wind Casino & Hotel, where untaxed slot machine profits provide our country's idea of amends for the Wounded Knee Massacre, I caught a ride to the airport in Rapid City. A few days later, the famous war photographer emailed to say he was safely back in Libya.

Eventually the Hoka Hey organizers announced the results: Eleven riders reached Nova Scotia within the 16-day time limit. Will Barclay crossed the finish line at 5:51 p.m. on August 19, posting a time of 14 days, 12 hours and 8 minutes. Frank Kelly arrived fourth, more than a day later. During the final stretch up the Eastern Seaboard, Hurricane Irene and an oddly out-of-place earthquake gave the stragglers some extra trouble, but another 41 riders completed the course with no deviations. Big Jim was listed as a non-finishing participant, as were Charles Laws, Whittany Crum, Elijah Whirlwind Horse and Gregory Shafer. A news release described a party back at Chester's, with the film crew on hand, but made no mention of any awards. Instead, the organizers said, tracking data and polygraph tests would help determine an eventual winner.

Last summer, 91 riders turned out for another running. Publicity materials promised, "If you didn't know your own mind before you start — you will have discovered what you are made of by the time you reach the finish line!!"

But the 2011 race has taken on the aura of legend. On the Internet Movie Database, Dave Roma's film is listed as a postproduction project called "Indians & Cowboys." The plot synopsis says: "A Sioux man from the Pine Ridge Indian Reservation, Jim Red Cloud has a vision that gathered people from different walks of life and sent them marching into a modern day frontier. His unique experiment teaches us of the consequences of the American Dream and its fractured past in a modern day context."

Despite the prophecy, E.B. Chester did not die on the racecourse. He lived, only to become a co-defendant in a lawsuit over the prize money. In federal district court in Arizona, Will Barclay charged Big Jim and his wife, as operators of an entity called the Medicine Show Land Trust, with breach of contract, slander, libel and conspiracy.

In his civil complaint, Barclay says he arrived at Chester's for a victory party in October 2011, expecting to collect his winnings of $250,000 and a new Harley. Instead, at an assembly of prize contenders, Big Jim described him as a CIA operative trained in "countermeasures" to defeat a polygraph exam, who "cheated my people, everyone that rode in that Hoka Hey including those that paid with their lives and everyone that has ever ridden a motorcycle."

Chester, for his part, denied any part in disqualifying Barclay. In court documents, he admitted little more than being a citizen of Arizona.

In a response filed in November 2012, Big Jim said the results of the polygraph had been inconclusive. Because passing the exam was a condition of winning, he wrote, Barclay did not qualify for the prize money. Big Jim did admit to describing Barclay as a CIA operative, based on Barclay's own boasts. Also, he admitted to saying that Barclay had "cheated his people and the riders of the Hoka Hey Challenge."

The trading of paperwork in court has been scheduled through the spring of 2014, with a trial to follow if the parties cannot work out a settlement.

As for the Lakota, the organizers have announced raising "several thousands of dollars" for the Red Cloud Humanitarian Fund. Records show the Internal Revenue Service has revoked the nonprofit status of a charity by that name, based in Pine Ridge, for failing to file tax records for three consecutive years.

Meanwhile, the next running of the Hoka Hey Motorcycle Challenge is soliciting riders for a 7,000-mile race from upstate New York through the Arctic. The entry fee is $1,000. The theme is "'Wolakota,' Walk in Peace."

Old New Yorkers, Newer Ones, and the Line Etched by Sept. 11

Time is the most challenging dimension for journalists. The business has its roots in speed and compression, and it's hard to take time's full measure—the simple fact that it changes everything—on deadline. That's why Mike Brick's "Old New Yorkers, Newer Ones, and a Line Etched by a Day of Disaster" is such a little miracle of a story, or, to be more precise, a big miracle that does its work in tight quarters. It's a 9/11 story, so at first its strength seems to be that it goes small on the most enormous of subjects. But that's deceptive, because what Mike Brick does in the span of about 1,500 words is keep upping the ante until he's written a 9/11 story that's about nothing less than time itself.

The New York Times lists the story's publication date as September 7, 2006, so the nature of its cause and occasion is crystal clear—it's a story meant to mark an impending milestone, the kind of thing that has been the stock-in-trade of daily newspapers since the invention of movable type. To pull it off, a reporter has only to be humane to the people he quotes and graceful in how he quotes them. All he has to do is find a way to say that "life goes on," and his job is done. But that's not what Mike does here, not exactly. Instead, he finds a way to say that if life goes on, so does death—and that everything is mortal, even tragedy.

He starts the story with time and with numbers, writing that in the five years since the planes came and the buildings fell and the people never came home from work, "645,416 babies were born and 304,773 people died. A half-million more people came from other countries than departed for them, and 800,000 more people left for the 50 states than came wide-eyed from them." Life would indeed seem to go on...except that what all those new additions and new arrivals wind up doing is burying what's most important to those who came before them.

"Five years on," Mike writes, "New York is a city of newcomers and survivors. And between them runs a line. The line makes for no conflict, no discernible tension; it works a quieter breach." It is the line between innocence and experience, between memory and forgetting—and, in the great achievement of "Old New Yorkers, Newer Ones, and a Line Etched by a Day of Disaster," it becomes Mike Brick's central character. In a story 42 paragraphs long, he mentions "the line" in 16, until those two words become a drumbeat, an abstraction that somehow gains the weedy permanence of a character profiled by Joseph Mitchell.

From beginning to end Mike is graceful and humane in spades, but saves his deepest compassion not for the experienced but rather for the innocent: "on the [line's] other side, you can feel like the new boyfriend at your girlfriend's family reunion the year somebody died—somebody young, somebody you never met."

It's tempting to read that sentence from the vantage of retrospective knowledge, as the presentiment of someone who was, and who will now always be, "somebody young." But all journalists come to learn that they're never going to get the space they need. Mike Brick always worked in a deeper and nearly invisible dimension, so he must have known, without having to be told, that neither do we get the time.

—Tom Junod

DATELINE: New York, New York

Five years ago, on Sept. 11, 2001, terrorists crashed two airliners into the World Trade Center. Downtown smelled like Coke cans and hair on fire. It was televised live.

In New York City, 2,749 people were killed. About eight million remained. Since that day, the numbers have changed.

The population grew by more than 134,000 from 2000 to 2005, the city's latest Planning Department calculations show. In that time, 645,416 babies were born and 304,773 people died. A half-million more people came from other countries than departed for them, and 800,000 more people left for the 50 states than came wide-eyed from them.

The meaning in the math is that today a great many New Yorkers lack firsthand knowledge of the city's critical modern moment.

Five years on, New York is a city of newcomers and survivors. And between them runs a line. The line makes for no conflict, no discernible tension; it works a quieter breach.

Borne of the routine comings and goings of urban life, of births and deaths, the line divides views of a singular moment. Across the line, consummately familiar events can appear contorted.

On one side, the newcomer side, a man seeks accounts of that day; on the other side a man withholds his account. On the newcomer side, a woman visits the absent towers to feel some connection; on the other side a woman feels connected, and then some.

On the side of those who lived in New York, you can share a sense of trauma both layered and ill-defined.

"It's like someone who has been in a war zone," said William Stockbridge, 50, a finance executive who was working downtown during the attack. "It's different."

On the other side, you can feel like the new boyfriend at your girlfriend's family reunion the year somebody died—somebody young, somebody you never met.

"You feel like you're on the outside," said Matthew Molnar, 26, a waiter in Williamsburg, Brooklyn, who lived in Middlesex County, N.J., in 2001. "You feel like you missed out on a little bit of history."

Newcomers and survivors: those terms ring harsh and blunt only because the line is so often unspoken. It runs soundless and invisible down Broadway from Harlem over the Williamsburg Bridge out to Coney Island and to Fresh Kills, up past the airports across the Grand Concourse into Yankee Stadium, through the bleachers where you can't drink beer anymore and up out of the park into the nighttime sky.

The line flashes into view on the city streets for moments at a time. When jet fighters buzz the skyscrapers for Fleet Week, some of the people below—the ones who were here on Sept. 11—flinch. More frequently, though, the line operates beneath the surface of conversations, of interactions, of transactions, of life. The line controls small things, controls the way people react to the phrase "and then Sept. 11 happened," as though a date on the calendar could "happen."

The line's contours emerge in conversations. Ask about the attack, and people will describe a sense of ownership.

"You either experienced it firsthand," said Amanda Spielman, 30, a graphic designer from Jackson Heights, Queens, who was in the city, "or you didn't."

Others describe that sense differently, but draw the line in the same place.

"I think for the people that seen it on TV, it is more painful than for the people who saw it here," said Paolo Gonzalez, 29, who manages a parking lot under the Brooklyn Bridge and who saw the attack. "For the other people it was real. If you was here, when the buildings came down the only thing you were thinking was, 'Run.'"

Across the line, the new arrivals recognize that sense of ownership.

"I've been told that I just don't get it, and that I could never understand what it was like to be there in New York on Sept. 11," said Laura Bassett, 27, who moved to the city from North Carolina after 2001. "I hate that five years later, people still debate which bystander is allowed to be more upset, the New Yorker or the American."

The line emerges perhaps most powerfully around the fallen towers, 2.06 acres of concrete known as Ground Zero. Because of the line, the site is a paradox, an emotional contradiction, a mass grave and a tourist attraction.

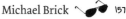

Some people feel so strongly about the place they cannot agree on an arrangement for listing the names of the dead; others feel so strongly about the place that they make sure to visit between Radio City Music Hall and the Statue of Liberty. Between those emotional poles is a middle ground, and the line runs through its center.

"People who moved to New York, everyone wanted to go down and see it," said Dede Minor, 51, a real estate broker who was in her office in Midtown on the day of the attack. "For New Yorkers, it was too real."

Jose Martias, 57, a construction worker who was drinking coffee near the East River when the attack began, said he knew why the newcomers visit the site.

"They don't understand it so they go down there to see the hole," Mr. Martias said. "It's an attraction to them, like going to the circus."

But across the line there is genuine emotional curiosity, a feeling that people in less cynical times used to call empathy.

"I didn't think I'd be that affected," said Leah Hamilton, 24, a logistics consultant who moved to Manhattan from Washington State last year. "But when I went to ground zero, it was the first time I've felt an emotional reaction like that to something I wasn't a part of. You feel the energy and you could feel the sadness."

The line can reach into the future, forging perceptions of New York and its destiny. Some new arrivals speak of the attack as a reason to come to the city.

"We felt like there was a lot of energy here," said Meg Glasser, 26, a student who moved to the East Village from Boston this year. "We wanted to be a part of it in some way."

But across the line, that sense of energy is tempered by standards for comparison.

"I know people who have been here a year or two, and they find New York fantastic," said Father Bernard, 67, a Roman Catholic monk who was born in Brooklyn and who goes by only that name. "They're right, but they didn't know the New York before."

The line reaches into the past as well, dividing memories. Each generation tells the next where they were when the bombs fell on Pearl Harbor, when the Kennedys and Martin Luther King were killed or when a space shuttle exploded, but a major act of destruction in a major American city creates more firsthand accounts.

Psychological studies suggest those accounts have played a role in drawing the line. After the attack, a group of academic researchers interviewed 1,500 people, including 550 in New York City, to gauge memories of detail, said Elizabeth Phelps, a professor of psychology and neural science at New York University. Proximity to Lower Manhattan during the attack, Dr. Phelps said, "increases your confidence in your memories, and your accuracy as well."

In a separate study, the researchers measured activity in parts of the brain connected to memory. With verbal cues, subjects were asked to conjure visions of the terror attack and of personal events from the summer of 2001. Only half registered a difference in neural activity.

"Those who did show a difference were, on average, in Washington Square Park," Dr. Phelps said. "Those who didn't were, on average, in Midtown."

Among those who have come to the city since 2001, the line dividing memories is undisputed.

"I had been there as a tourist to the World Trade Center, so I have memories," said Marielle Solan, 22, a photographer who moved to the city from Delaware this year. "But obviously I can't have any sense of what it was like. Every Sept, 11, you get a sense of fear and depression, but in terms of actual visceral reactions, I don't really have that."

The new arrivals have found a conspicuous void of shared memory.

"I'm amazed because it was such a big event, and people never mention it," said Deenah Vollmer, 20, who moved to the city last year. "When you do mention it, everyone has these crazy intense stories."

Across the line, many of those who lived in the city hold their memories close.

"The people I already knew know my stories from that day, so there's no need to repeat them," said Ms. Spielman, the graphic designer. "The new people I've met don't ask me. It's not something I bring up."

But each year the calendar brings it up. Alexandria Lambert, 28, who works as an administrative assistant, sees the line run through the center of her office. Each year, a co-worker who witnessed the attack asks for the day off, and each year a boss who did not declines the request.

"His point of view is, 'Don't let it get you down,'" Ms. Lambert said, "but she just doesn't want to be here."

Reporting for this article was contributed by Sarah Garland, Kate Hammer, Colin Moynihan and Conrad Mulcahy.

— *The New York Times*, September 7, 2006

Life Without Parole for Killer of a Police Officer

O f all the things about reporting and writing that technology has changed, deadline writing is one of the few things that it has intensified rather than destroyed. Writing well and writing fast always has been part of the job. (In fact, it's one of my favorite parts.) But the acceleration caused by the new technologies has produced a culture within journalism in which you're never not on deadline. Baseball writers have to do blog posts during the game. Reporters covering political campaigns have to tweet from every gelid cornfield in Iowa. It used to be that you were on deadline, and then you weren't. There is no such thing as being off deadline anymore.

Look at what Michael Brick does here, in his account of the sentencing of a murder suspect in a courthouse in the Bronx. You can smell the crowded humanity of the gallery and the aroma of decades of old varnish on the wood. You can hear a man's life being lost, without parole, in the shuffling of papers. And then there's this, about the convicted man, which is pure Brick:

"With his long legs stretched out to cross at the ankles, his gaze like a vacant lot…"

Writing well and writing fast always has been what newspaper reporters have for poetry. If I had to guess, and if he's anything like me, I'd say Brick didn't know how good that passage was until he saw it in the newspaper. The deadline is a muse well-camouflaged. You just have to listen very closely for her song because, goddamn, it passes quickly.

—Charles P. Pierce

DATELINE: Brooklyn, New York

With his long legs stretched out to cross at the ankles, his gaze like a vacant lot, Allan Cameron was sentenced yesterday to life in prison with no chance of parole for murdering a police officer during a midnight car chase through the streets of Flatbush.

Mr. Cameron, 29, protested his fate.

"The only thing I'm guilty of today, Your Honor," he told the judge just before the sentence was handed down, "is being young, black and poor."

But a jury had found differently. In the predawn hours of Nov. 28, 2005, prosecutors said, Mr. Cameron ran a stoplight in his red Infiniti. He was on probation for running from the police, wanted on assault charges and carrying a 9-millimeter handgun.

His traffic violation drew the attention of Officer Dillon Stewart, 35, prosecutors said. A high-speed chase described a rough rectangle around the neighborhood. The cars screeched to a sidelong stop. There were six shots. Officer Stewart was struck through the heart as he sat in the driver's seat; he was dead within hours.

No one save perhaps Officer Stewart saw the gunman's face. But with a wealth of forensic evidence, Mr. Cameron was convicted of first-degree murder. Uniformed officers filled the courtroom for his trial, stared him down and applauded a ruling that did not go his way.

When his time of reckoning came, the officers returned. This time they filled an outsized ceremonial courtroom in State Supreme Court in Brooklyn past its capacity of 164 and spilled into the hallway.

TV reporters watched from the padded swivel chairs of the jury box. Mr. Cameron's family watched from the second row of the gallery. His defense lawyers told them to hold out hope for a successful appeal.

Justice Albert Tomei surveyed the courtroom with his customary frown.

"I don't want any clapping, I don't want any screaming—anything," he said. "I'm going to do this in a dignified manner."

Mr. Cameron, in a black suit, was led into the courtroom. His handcuffs were left in place.

Officer Stewart's relatives watched from the center of the gallery. They wore funeral clothes. His sister, Sheryl Campbell-Julien, spoke of the night he was killed.

"I dreamt that the skies opened up and out came a beam of light and through the light the voice of my brother saying, 'I love you,'" she told the court. Reading through tears from a composition book, she told of praying for his life, of lost plans to watch their children grow together and of "a void in my heart."

Their mother, Winifred Fleming, spoke of "a thousand things I wish I had said to him when he was here."

And his widow, Leslyn Stewart, loudly and forcefully asked for the maximum penalty, repeating over and over "life without parole."

"It is not how he died but how he lived," she said, "that made him a true hero."

A lawyer for Mr. Cameron, John Burke, offered condolences to the Stewart family. He asked for a lesser term, arguing that the killing had not been premeditated.

He spoke of the nation's world-beating incarceration rates and the city's tactics against petty crime, which can lead to confrontations between officers and civilians.

Then Mr. Cameron stood and protested the jury's verdict. As he spoke, he seemed unable to pronounce the victim's name.

"I'm very sorry for your losses," he said, "but I did not have anything to do with Officer Stew—Officer Stroh's death, and the truth is going to come out one of these days." His lawyer suggested at the trial that the fatal shot could have been fired by another officer during the chase.

Saying that the denial had betrayed a lack of remorse, Justice Tomei prescribed the maximum penalty. He spoke of a century's progress in science, lamenting that "when it comes to humanity and the way we treat each other, we are still in the dark ages."

"Hopefully one day we as humanity will emerge from the darkness," Justice Tomei said, "and we will not see the likes of Allan Cameron and his ilk praying at the altar of violence and killing machines."

Outside, there was applause. The uniformed officers descended the escalators, an uninterrupted stream of royal blue, back to the streets of Brooklyn and the coming night.

—*The New York Times*, November 9, 2007

Given Five Extra Years to Live, New Yorkers Look for a Catch

A ll newsrooms, tiny or more august, are driven by the same thing: daily desperation. We like to talk a bunch about the First Amendment and our role in a vibrant democracy. We fancy ourselves crusaders or truth tellers.

Whatever.

What enlivens us really is stone-cold fear of not having enough copy for the next day's edition. Which is why, one Thanksgiving week in the newsroom of The New York Times, we found ourselves in a panic because we had no heartwarming story of coming together in gratitude and harmony. We were out of good ideas. Shit, we were out of bad ideas. And for a long while.

The homeless; the war-damaged; the incarcerated; the old timers and the newly sober; the freshly arrived immigrant and the dug-in New York stalwart. Done and done and done. And then done over—reheated turkeys, one might say.

But a Thursday edition beckoned, and so we said what we so often said in such moments of acute and embarrassing need: "What about Brick?"

"Right!" said someone.

"Genius!" said someone else.

"Well, it's a start," said the resident realist.

It all came together quickly, which of course foretold what would come next.

Let's do a story about everyone's worst Thanksgiving ever. The feuds. The family fractures. The burnt birds. The long silences and the short fist-fights. And let's get Brick to write it up.

Mike had some of the requisite qualifications: he was fast; he had wit; he was a good soldier. Oh, and most importantly, he had zero seniority and absolutely no kids, so fuck him if he already had Thanksgiving plans.

Mike took the assignment pretty well. Or faked it pretty good. And then, 48 hours later, he handed in his typed-up revenge.

Mike's story about the worst Thanksgivings ever had some tales of good intentions gone horribly wrong, of expensive food rendered inedible, of marriages ended and lifespans shortened.

But its central character was an aggrieved reporter who was living out his worst Thanksgiving ever—reporting out the half-baked, soul-crushing story idea hatched by a set of desperate New York Times editors with no good Thanksgiving story in their cupboard.

Truth be told, it was pretty hilarious. Equally true was the fact that it was never going to run. The story was spiked.

Mike, if nothing else, is spectacularly earnest, and he took the defeat hard. The story, an act of dignified defiance, wasn't a bad piece of writing, either. He thought us cowards, I believe. And, 15 years or so on, it's my duty to report he wasn't wrong.

So, I have no link for you here. My favorite Mike Brick story is one that was never published. But I invite you to consider that this is appropriate and righteous. Mike's best work has been done off stage, with his kids and his wife and his parents and his brother, with his guitar and his song notebooks and his friends, with his chemo and his giant heart. The stories were not formally recorded or publicly chronicled. They will live on by word of mouth, shared anecdotally and cherished forever, acts of heroism and plain decency both.

Need something?

"What about Brick?"

Indeed.

—Joseph Sexton

DATELINE: New York, New York

Let's play a game.

Because a dim light warmed us yesterday, and we could go outdoors without a jacket, and because we are younger than we were last week, let's play.

The city told us we have time. Compared with New Yorkers just one decade ago, we have 6.8 more years if we are boys and 3.2 more years if we are girls, the Department of Health and Mental Hygiene said this week in a study of life expectancy rates.

So call it five years, and let's pretend we can follow our whims. It is found time. It is not the free time that money can buy, or the five years the doctor gives someone with an unspeakable disease. Just extra time. Let's decide what to do with it.

This being New York, though, an examination of this sudden temporal windfall is expected. It all sounds a little suspicious.

"What am I, old, though?" asked Howard Grandison, who spent part of yesterday afternoon lounging on the concrete steps in Union Square. He wanted to clarify the specific terms. He wanted to know the rules of the game. It's only fair.

That point was amplified by Ralf Itzwerth, from Sydney, Australia, who was visiting New York for the first time, staring down from the observation deck of the Empire State Building at the tiny-looking people with the five extra years.

"Just living long doesn't mean that you're happy," Mr. Itzwerth said. "You might limp through life on one leg. You might live two years longer on your respirator with your lung cancer."

This whole five-extra-years business will cause other problems, too, said Sean Keenan, 32, a firefighter, who was standing in front of a firehouse on West 37th Street. "Try to collect Social Security," Firefighter Keenan said. "I'm sure I'll be working."

Time out. This game cannot get started until New Yorkers accept that they have five extra years, and dream. Let's just think about five good years.

We could marry. Or divorce. We could spend it underwater (more about that in a moment). We could travel, or just while away the afternoon sitting on a fire-hose connector on 17th Street clutching a cigarette. That is what a man who gave his name as Bob Jones—and who was kind enough to mention that "Bob Jones" is also the name of a university, as if to signal that he was giving a fake name—was doing yesterday. He did not have trouble finding a reserve of gratitude for five extra years.

"I'm going to tell you what I'm going to say: Thank God," said Bob Jones, if that is his real name. "What would I do with it? Keep on praying, keep on praying, keep on praying. All right. I came a long way."

Philip Chadwick, a graphic designer who was reading the newspaper in Union Square, said: "When it's time to go, it's time to go. But I don't think anyone would turn it down."

But those are heavy thoughts. And that is not the point of this game. With all the stress and worry and fussing, it seems as if New Yorkers ought to be dying younger every day, not having their life expectancies extended. So let's play.

Lenny Speregen, 43, a commercial diver who lives in Brooklyn, bought a glass of carrot juice in Midtown yesterday, not so much because it might help him live longer but because it might help him see more clearly when he is down in the depths of the Hudson River.

You have five extra years, Mr. Speregen. Whatever will you do? "Hopefully spend it underwater," Mr. Speregen said, describing how when he's submerged, the only person he worries about is whoever is on the boat or shore monitoring his equipment.

"It's the most stress-free environment," he added.

You have five years, David Mark Patterson. Yesterday you were in Union Square, where you read a book. What will you do with your five extra years?

"I am going to spend five more years wandering the streets looking for nuances and intricacies to turn into tangible data— " Mr. Patterson said. He was apparently starting a joke, making fun of the statisticians who tell New Yorkers how long they will live, but he was interrupted, and implored to play the game. "I would go around town doing guerrilla sculptures," he said.

Fine. And Bryan D. Johnson will relax. Coleen Bradley will write to express herself artistically instead of writing to please her bosses and make money. Ron Cohen will retire and ride his mountain bike. Sean Ross will drink heavily, unless he was kidding.

And Robert Presti, 38, the owner of Simply Natural, a juice and vitamin supplement shop, will move more slowly and deliberately. "With that extra five years, all the stresses New Yorkers are under to do things quickly, we'll be able to take it slow," Mr. Presti said. "At least as slow as the rest of the country takes it. It'll all come out in the wash eventually."

What game should we play next? We have some extra time left.

—*The New York Times*, April 23, 2003

The Distributor

I saw this story as a meditation on the role of seemingly random circumstances in ordinary lives, the way seemingly small coincidences can upend things. I was trying to use all the backstory to establish the ordinariness and promise of the characters. And ultimately I wanted to set up Johnny and Ricky as mirror images, very similar characters with slight differences that send them down very different paths on a collision course.

The variety of reactions I've gotten convinces me that I at least achieved a challenging piece of writing. A few hours before I got your note, an editor at Penthouse, of all places, wrote to tell me the piece needs "a real ending."

—Michael Brick, in a 2010 email to a friend,
lamenting the vicissitudes of the magazine industry

Johnny Goosey led his party past the Tip Top dry cleaners to the back of a low-slung shopping center, through a recessed door into a candlelit restaurant. The Swiss timepiece on his wrist read 10 o'clock, already late for dinner by the standards of Austin, Texas, where summertime visits a long slow idyll. Hours past sundown on the last Monday in June 2009, the temperature was holding steady near 80 degrees. The big music festivals were done, the state legislature was out of session and most of the 39,000 undergraduates of the University of Texas had gone home to Houston and Dallas, Cuero and Abilene, countless small towns and ranches across the state.

At 21, Goosey had graduated high school and college ahead of his classmates. In the year since his last semester on campus, he had held no formal job. His six-foot frame, trim from kayaking and cycling, was starting to regain its childhood paunch. His manner was relaxed, his posture slumped, his gait unhurried. He cut his own hair. Aside from the IWC watch, his wardrobe was unflashy to the point of raggedness, cargo shorts, flip-flops.

Escorting his girlfriend, a pretty brunette with vaguely Asian features, Goosey selected a center table. He skipped his customary Manhattan and ordered dayboat scallops on butternut squash puree, cervena venison on elf mushrooms, veal sweetbreads on gnocchi with cherry tomatoes and more. The chef provided complimentary meringue, crème brulee and el rey chocolate cake for desserts.

Goosey raised a glass of red wine. He was earning enough to afford these dinners at Wink, Buenos Aires and the Driskill Hotel, where he seemed to have a standing reservation. In a span of a little more than three years, he had earned his history degree with honors, romanced the love of his life and kept close ties with his family, all while building an operation to handle more than $30,000 a week worth of exotic designer marijuana. Despite the geographic proximity to the violent smuggling gangs of the Mexican border, his stature as a successful distributor seemed relatively safe, based on a network of domestic greenhouses on the supply side and clean-cut college men on the retail side. Still, he was unsure what to make of his youngest dealer, a 19-year-old high school dropout, the son of a university instructor living a few blocks from his off-campus apartment. The dealer's name was Ricky Thompson. Goosey called him "the dumbass."

Within a month, Goosey and his girlfriend would be shot dead in their apartment. At first, investigators would describe the killings as potentially random, spooking parents across the state. Then court filings would portray a limited picture of Goosey's dealings with marijuana, enough to stir imaginations. Later, Thompson would plead guilty to murder.

But for now a toast was raised.

"Remember these moments for what they are," Goosey told his friends. "Happiness only comes once in awhile."

* * *

Above a certain social stratum in Houston, the Goosey name has been prominent for years. Dr. John D. Goosey promotes his laser vision correction practice to a national clientele, travels a worldwide lecture circuit and counts numerous textbook credits among his accomplishments. Balding, tennis-fit and stern of manner, he works long hours while his wife, Claire, makes the charitable fundraising scene.

"She's lively and funny," says Kent Schaffer, a longtime family friend. "He's a very serious guy."

In a bedroom community not far from the museum district of central Houston, the Gooseys indulged their two children, providing a safe place to host sleepovers, play ping-pong and exercise in the home gym. Their fridge was stocked with snacks. Their pool had a slide and a waterfall. Their daughter finished high school early, rejected material concerns and moved to London to pursue art.

Their son, named John Forest after his grandfathers, grew up chubby, with dark unruly ringlets, big Lebanese eyes and a small scar on his cheek, the result of an attempt to retrieve a stolen morsel from his Labrador. Everyone called him Johnny. As a child, he attended the Annunciation Orthodox School, where annual tuition costs $15,800. He was a mischievous boy, setting off fireworks and playing practical jokes. He wore his outgrown uniform nearly every day of his freshman year at Mirabeau B. Lamar High School, a public business magnet. He refused to buy new sneakers, even when carpool companions rolled down their windows and complained. He developed an abiding affection for grotesque artwork, particularly a drawing of a big-headed pterodactyl on stick legs. He had tiny, inscrutable handwriting, a compressed hybrid of print and script. He had little luck with girls.

"In high school, Johnny was the entertainer," a friend would later recall, "cracking jokes, always scheming, trying to pick up people, pushing the limit."

During long sessions in a rented studio space, recording funk riffs on his bass guitar, he tripped mushrooms and smoked marijuana. One of his oldest friends from grade school was a dealer. Goosey would eventually let lapse his musical inclinations, but never his marijuana connections.

From a young age, he seemed unchallenged even by the high standards of exclusive schools. In classes from public speaking to algebra, he goofed off and aced the exams. After his older sister graduated in three years, he started sitting away from his friends in class, attending summer school and locking himself in his room to study. He earned his diploma in August 2004, a year before his classmates. He enrolled at the University of Houston, making A's in nearly every subject, while attending the high school party circuit.

"What are you doing here, college boy?" his old friends sometimes joked.

When his classmates finished high school, Goosey transferred to the University of Texas at Austin, immersing himself in the study of foreign cultures, blues music and philosophy, including a class called "Knowledge and Reality." On his application form, he indicated an intention to teach middle school, a passing fancy. Though he would return home to visit, inviting friends to drink beer and philosophize with his father, he quickly sought to define himself against his privileged upbringing. He traded out the BMW presented at high school graduation for a paint-splattered 2002 Prius.

"What does it tell a 17-year-old boy," Goosey asked a friend, "when your dad gives you a $70,000 toy?"

In class, he kept up honor roll grades, using flash cards and visiting his professors. "He was a brilliant student in every way," said

Syed Hyder, the instructor of a class on Sufism and Islamic Mysticism. Goosey recited Romantic poetry with ease, and developed a brief fascination with Moloch, the rebel angel of "Paradise Lost."

Outside of class, his marijuana business was hardly unusual. At first, it was hardly even a business. Like generations of college students, he started selling quarter-ounce bags to a small circle of friends and vouched acquaintances, charging just enough to underwrite his own habit. "You didn't have to be dealing with shadesters to set pot in West Campus," an acquaintance would later recall. "He was just making money. It was easy."

* * *

In April 2006, when Goosey was a sophomore at UT, he accompanied some friends to the Villas on Guadalupe, sharing Parliament Lights on the balcony with Stacy Marie Barnett, a design student one year his senior. Minutes turned to hours, long enough for the two of them to be missed. They had much to discuss: Growing up in the same neighborhood, graduating the same high school, mutual friends. Barnett was naturally pretty, with unpainted lips, dark eyes and brown hair, which she cut into a bob every few months to make wigs for cancer patients. She stood five feet three-quarters of an inch tall, weighed a hundred pounds and went by the nickname Staceum, pronounced "Stay-some."

Her dress was conservative, brown and gray assemblages from the Gap matched with tasseled slip-on shoes, chunky rings, colorful bracelets and sterling silver necklaces worn despite her eczema. As an affectation, she sometimes put on white square Jackie O glasses and carried an outsize purse on her elbow.

For a pretty girl, she was camera shy. She cackled. She talked with her hands, holding wiggling fingers face down at chest level as though trying to conjure her next thought from some unseen cauldron. She had been raised in a renovated house with her name etched in the garage concrete, the younger of two half-Chinese daughters of a tile company executive. She had marched in the Fourth of July fire truck parade, enrolled in gifted and talented classes and come in for discipline only once, at age three, for refusal to take a bath. She had joined softball, volleyball, swim and soccer teams, severed the altar at Sunday Mass and spent her allowance on poetry volumes at Half Price Books. She kept voluminous journals, recording her thoughts with perfectly rounded letters in Pilot Precise V5 Extra Fine ink. At age 14, she had composed a 17-line work of free verse called "Areeoleei," which concluded:

> *Behind her concealed wisdom*
> *Lies the face of a girl*
> *Waiting, as her destiny*
> *Approaches her loneliness*
> *And leads her, as they dance*
> *Whispering their imperfections through each other's*
> *Impeccable nature.*

At high school parties, she tried marijuana but held back with a "You guy-ees" when anything heavier was proposed. She was a lightweight. At the home of a friend with permissive parents, she had once spun recent dental work into an excuse to decline a hit: "You guy-ees, I can't smoke, I'll suck my wisdom teeth out."

She had taken highest honors at Lamar High School. She was reasonably well traveled, with a taste for art museums on the high end, Miley Cyrus Twitter postings on the low end and little of note in between. She drank tall nonfat lattes, made mix CDs, watched "Sex and the City" marathons and quoted Le Corbusier.

Denied entry to the competitive architecture school at the University of Texas, she had scored fourteen A's and one B in her first year as a liberal arts student, earning a transfer. To instructors, she demonstrated a precocious sense of emotional expression through design. She had recently broken up with her late-sleeping boyfriend, resolving to remain single for a year.

That night, Goosey made a strong impression. Quoting poetry, talking politics and flashing a quarterback smile: This was not the chunky prankster so easily ignored in high school. Barnett agreed to see him again. Soon they were drawing complaints for public displays of affection.

"What happened to the single-for-a-year thing?" one friend remembers asking.

"It's out the window," Barnett said.

* * *

In the fall of 2006, Goosey studied Spanish abroad at the Universidad de Alicante. When he returned, Barnett was waiting. So was a new opportunity: An acquaintance, a marijuana supplier operating at a higher level, had just been arrested. Through an intermediary, Goosey was offered a chance to inherit the supplier's network of greenhouse growers spread between Austin and Houston. Though he had plenty of pocket money, something had left him unsatisfied, something about all those nights out in the restaurants, all those friends dropping their parents' credit cards on the table.

"Johnny didn't do it for the money," a friend would later recall. "He did it because he wanted to be independent, and not take from his parents."

Goosey started making day trips to Houston, a five-hour round trip, for bags of hydroponic marijuana worth $4,500 to $5,500 a pound, strains with names like purple, skunk, black widow and white widow.

Across the state, drug enforcement agencies had more pressing concerns. Last year, federal agents seized 1.2 million pounds of marijuana, three times the amount taken in California, orders of magnitude more than most other states. Mexican, Colombian and Dominican smuggling operations, responsible for countless killings, package air, land and sea shipments of marijuana with dangerously addictive drugs such as methamphetamine, cocaine and heroin for nationwide distribution. Development of the four-lane La Entrada al Pacifico highway, from Topolobampo in the cartel stronghold of western Mexico through the border town of Presidio into the distribution hub of Midland-Odessa, promises to divert more drug traffic overland through Texas, away from the congested Port of Los Angeles.

In Austin, the college-age population provides steady demand. "Marijuana has always been an issue," says one senior official of the Austin Police Department. "You could pick Anytown U.S.A., and you're going to find a drug presence near educational organizations."

With no concession to nationwide efforts at decriminalization, medical licensing and other legal outlets for personal use, the business remains fully underground, competitive and deadly. Field-grown marijuana imported by the Sinaloa and Gulf Coast cartels moves in quantities of hundreds of pounds to prison gangs such as the Texas Syndicate, the Mexican Mafia and the Tango Blast, which employ local affiliates of the Bloods and the Crips to distribute ten-pound packages. Depending on the operation, one or two lower levels of hustlers break the product down for sale, where profitability spreads thin.

Separate, domestic greenhouse supply chains produce much of the expensive, potent marijuana popular among discerning young professional types. At the height of his operation, Goosey was selling about a pound a week to each of about six customers, who in turn sold smaller quantities. "With how smart he was, it just blew up," one friend would later recall. "The better he got at it, the fewer people he dealt with."

All of his customers were respectably dressed, easygoing, late-college-aged men, all but one.

"Hold on," Goosey announced, interrupting an afternoon of video games. "The dumbass is coming over."

* * *

By the end of 2007, Goosey was living in an upscale condominium, though the pterodactyl portrait, a work of art most generously described as abstract, still held a prominent place on his wall. His customers usually took a seat on the couch, smoked a joint and watched some TV. Not this one. James Richard Thompson Jr. lingered in the alcove, scrawny, nervous-looking and unimpressive, dressed as some aspiring gangsta in a throwback cap and bling watch.

"This is Ricky," Goosey said.

Nobody got up. Thompson didn't stick around too long.

"He looks young," one of Goosey's friends said. "Is he in high school?"

"Yeah," Goosey said. "I think so."

But Thompson was not in high school. After his parents divorced in 2003, when he was twelve, Thompson had moved into a small house in West Campus with his mother, an anthropology lecturer at the University of Texas. As a child, he was short, with bushy eyebrows, a slight overbite and twin birthmarks below his left eye. He played Little League baseball, rode a skateboard and rose to the rank of Eagle Scout. He loved camping.

When his mother remarried, Thompson joined his father in Lakeway, an exurban city of stone mini-mansions with in-ground pools, fountains and wandering deer. He dropped out of Lake Travis High School, smoked marijuana and abused cough syrup. He quit a series of menial jobs at a grocery store, a Chik-fil-A and Pao's Mandarin Delivery.

Outside of work, Thompson lifted weights, took supplements and tried to bulk up. He wore fake diamond earrings. He took in a pit bull. He drove a BMW. Among his peers, he spoke of little other than selling drugs. Around Lakeway, where three main suppliers dominate the trade, he always seemed to have a wider variety of marijuana. Still, he could never figure out how to take advantage. Though he kept quiet about his supplier, he was indiscriminate about his clientele. He was forever complaining about high school kids making tiny purchases or failing to pay up. He found plenty of small-time trouble.

On a weeknight in May 2008, Thompson and two other teenagers broke into the poolside bar at the Lakeway Inn, stole several bottles of liquor and stashed them in the trunk. Then they stole an iPod from a car in the parking lot. Then they started carting off televisions from the cabana. At some point they realized Thompson had locked his keys in the trunk. They called a pop-a-lock service. A police officer showed up instead. The police officer opened the trunk. Thompson agreed to testify against his friends.

"He acted like a hotshot, but unsure of himself at the same time," one of the young men arrested that night would later recall. "Always trying to be on top, but never knowing how to get there."

* * *

In the summer of 2008, Barnett rented a one-bedroom apartment at the Preservation Square Condominiums, promoted as "the jewel of West Campus." Goosey, whose degree plan was all but complete, moved in with Barnett, enrolling in a biology class called "Native Plants."

With her eye for design, Barnett assembled a tasteful starter apartment, decorating the living room with matching brown furniture, a flat-screen television and a polychrome rug resembling the work of Jackson Pollack. She found room for the pterodactyl drawing. In the kitchen, she allowed Goosey to store no more than an ounce of marijuana in a Tupperware container for personal use. At her insistence, his sales supply remained outside, stashed in the trunk of his Prius. As Barnett finished her senior year, earning mostly A's and trying to secure a job back home in Houston, Goosey let the date for the law school admission test come and go. She urged him to find legitimate work, to a point.

"Even though she wasn't happy with Johnny dealing, she adapted to it," a friend would later recall. "It was almost like it would be too much rocking the boat to say, 'If you don't stop dealing, you can't be my boyfriend.'"

In the fall of 2008, Goosey confronted the first ripple in his business. Thompson claimed he had been robbed of a pound of marijuana, worth about $5,000. After consulting a few close friends, Goosey agreed to front Thompson another pound to work off the debt. Over the next few months, Thompson repaid a little more than $1,000. Then, in the early summer of 2009, Thompson told Goosey he had been robbed again, bringing the debt to about $8,500. But out on Lakeway, Thompson was telling a different story.

* * *

Not far from Lake Travis, a retired IRS worker and roadie named Charles Cotton keeps a musty house full of burning incense, empty cat litter boxes and collectible hardbacks. Cotton has long white hair, a white beard and the guileless manner of a lifelong hippie. He favors torn hats and camouflage shorts. Though his telephone does not work, he is known for his solicitous hospitality, his readiness to put the Incredible Hulk on television and pass around beers.

As Cotton tells it, the son of a friend first introduced Thompson in the fall of 2008. Thompson, who seemed polite and reserved, walked around Cotton's blue couch, took a seat near the leather-bound books and turned down a beer, saying he had water in his car. He

spoke openly of his troubles as a small-time marijuana dealer, said he was trying to pay off debts and "go legit." He claimed a disgruntled customer had shown up outside his apartment yelling "Ricky's a drug dealer" over and over. Hearing sirens, Thompson had disposed of thousands of dollars worth of marijuana in a dumpster. Though his story seemed incredible, he inspired sympathy.

After that first visit, Thompson kept coming back every month. One time he wore a suit and tie, said he had found work as a cutlery salesman. Cotton let him practice his sales pitch, then gave him a hundred and fifty dollars for pruning shears and a knife, which later arrived by mail. Early in the summer, Thompson asked Cotton for $3,000. And in the middle of July, a police report shows, he asked to borrow a .22-caliber handgun.

* * *

"What should I do?" Goosey asked a friend. "He owes me a lot of money, and he's lying to me."

By mid-July, Barnett, who had spent the summer volunteering at an art museum, was packing her belongings for a move home to Houston. Her degree was finished, and her lease was about to expire. Goosey was sending mixed signals, one minute calling friends to discuss a marriage proposal, the next minute searching online for a new kayak and an apartment near the lake in Austin.

As he sat in the apartment talking over his options, a friend would later recall, Goosey seemed perplexed. "Maybe after I move, I just won't talk to him," he went on. He wondered aloud: *Two robberies? Was Thompson too dumb to think of a different lie? Was he crazy?*

On Friday, July 17, Barnett left town for a weekend rave, one last blowout before the move home. She bought new sunglasses at Nordstrom, braided her hair into pigtails and lost herself in the music. She was dancing to no pattern, covered in sweat, radiant from broken glow sticks. After the concert, she drove back to a rented country house for an after-party, blasting the song "Might Like You Better." She sat by an upstairs window for hours, peering out at the gathering crowd, at the stars, at the lasers playing off the canopy of trees under the nighttime sky.

Back in Austin, Goosey was getting lonely, drunk, agitated.

"He was like, 'I can't wait 'til she gets back,'" a friend would later recall. "'She keeps me in line.'"

Over the weekend, while Barnett was away, Goosey called Thompson's cell phone 19 times, a police report would later show. The calls went unanswered.

On Monday morning, as Thompson considered how to respond to the calls to his cell phone, his parents were otherwise engaged. They met in the presence of a lawyer to discuss some unpaid child support. A settlement was negotiated, with a payment plan. For his own debts, Thompson made no such arrangement.

At 6:49 p.m., Monday evening, Goosey took a three-minute call from Thompson's cell phone number, a police report shows. Later that night, he brought Barnett to meet some friends at an Argentine restaurant. He ordered pork tenderloin medallions with chimichurri sauce, green beans and Yukon Gold mashed potatoes. Barnett ordered fish.

Goosey raised another toast, this time to serendipity. He was in good spirits, anticipating some resolution to his concern, a friend would later recall. The group ordered five desserts.

"Oh, the $8,500 kid sent me a text," Goosey announced. "He said he was out to dinner with his mom, which was probably a lie, but he said he's going to call me tomorrow."

After dinner, they smoked cigarettes and drank cappuccino. One of their friends stayed overnight. Barnett went straight to bed. Goosey turned on a cartoon.

In the morning the sky was clear. It was already eighty degrees. Barnett asked a friend to drop off some cardboard moving boxes. Goosey sent a friend a playful text message, nothing but question marks. Their overnight guest would later recall walking out past a slight, unremarkable figure in a short-sleeve shirt, calm, quiet, unstartled, staring off into the middle distance, lingering on the wooden landing as though unsure to knock, carrying something heavy.

—*Ten Spurs*, Vol. 5, 2011

ACKNOWLEDGEMENTS

This anthology was compiled by friends of Michael Brick who hope his work will live on. It would not exist without the gracious help of Mike Sager, Dean Baquet, David E. McCraw, Mike Wilson and Nancy Barnes. Special thanks also goes to Kevin Robbins and the following contributors:

Andy Newman has been reporting and blogging local news for *The New York Times* since 1995. He lives in Brooklyn.

Michael Kruse, formerly of the *Tampa Bay Times*, is a senior staff writer for Politico. His work has appeared in *Grantland* and *Outside*.

Thomas Lake covers politics for CNN Digital. He has also written for *Sports Illustrated*, *The Guardian* and *The Washington Post*.

Ben Montgomery is a senior writer at the *Tampa Bay Times*. He lives in Tampa with his wife and three children.

Tony Rehagen is a freelance writer living in Atlanta.

Wright Thompson is a senior writer for *ESPN The Magazine*. He splits time between Connecticut and Mississippi.

Justin Heckert is a magazine writer living in Indianapolis. His stories have appeared in a variety of publications.

Chris Jones is a reporter and aspiring screenwriter. He lives in Port Hope, Ontario.

Erin Sullivan is former writer for the *Tampa Bay Times*. She lives in Tampa with her husband and daughter.

Mike Wilson is the editor of *The Dallas Morning News*.

Michael Wilson has been a reporter for *The New York Times* since 2002, and currently writes the column "Crime Scene."

Charles McNair's novels are *Land O' Goshen* and *Pickett's Charge*. He lives in Bogotá, Colombia, and writes a travel column for *Paste Magazine*, where he was Books Editor for 10 years.

Tommy Tomlinson is a contributing writer for ESPN and author of the upcoming memoir *The Elephant In the Room*. He lives in Charlotte.

Amy Wallace is *Los Angeles* magazine's editor-at-large and a correspondent for *GQ*. She lives in Pasadena.

Michael J. Mooney writes for *D Magazine*, *GQ*, and *ESPN The Magazine*. He lives in Dallas.

Joe Sexton worked with Mike during his 25 years at the *New York Times*.

Gary Smith is a former *Sports Illustrated* writer. He lives in South Carolina.

Michael Paterniti is a correspondent for *GQ*, and the author of several books. He lives in Portland, Maine.

Charles P. Pierce is a writer-at-large for *Esquire* and the author of four books. He lives near Boston.

Kurt Eichenwald is a senior writer for *Newsweek*, a contributing editor at *Vanity Fair*, and a *New York Times* bestselling author of four books.

Tom Junod has been a writer-at-large at *Esquire* for 18 years.

John Schwartz is a science reporter at *The New York Times*. He first met Mike Brick when they were part of the newspaper's Enron team.

Lena Price works as a fundraiser for a youth homeless shelter in Dallas. She studied journalism at UT Austin, where she was fortunate to stumble into a job as Michael Brick's research assistant for *Saving the School*.

Dan Barry is a reporter and columnist for *The New York Times*, and the author of four books.

ABOUT THE AUTHOR

Michael Brick, a senior writer for the *Houston Chronicle*, is the author of *Saving the School: The True Story of a Principal, a Teacher, a Coach, a Bunch of Kids and a Year in the Crosshairs of Education Reform*, a narrative nonfiction account of the effort to restore a troubled high school to its place as the heart of an inner city neighborhood in Texas. He is also the author of *The Big Race*, the story of a transcontinental motorcycle rally.

His feature stories have appeared in *Harper's*, *The New Republic*, *Newsweek* and *Sports Illustrated*. He previously worked as a reporter and sportswriter at *The New York Times*, where his assignments included the construction of Torre Mayor in Mexico City , the collapse of Enron, the aftermath of Hurricane Katrina, summer in a bar on Coney Island and a yearlong series on adventure sports.

Brick, who lived with his wife and children in Austin, died February 8, 2016, from colon cancer. He was 41.

ABOUT THE PUBLISHER

The Sager Group was founded in 1984. In 2012 it was chartered as a multi-media artists' and writers' consortium, with the intent of empowering those who make art—an umbrella beneath which makers can pursue, and profit from, their craft directly, without gatekeepers. TSG publishes eBooks and paper books; manages musical acts and produces live shows; ministers to artists and provides modest grants; and produces documentary, feature and web-based films. By harnessing the means of production, The Sager Group helps artists help themselves. For more information, please see www.TheSagerGroup.Net.

That was a good fucking taco.
—Michael Brick, January 9, 2016

Made in the USA
Columbia, SC
27 July 2019